A WORLD BANK STUDY

Old Risks, New Solutions, or Is It the Other Way Around?

Gero Verheyen and Edith Quintrell, editors

THE WORLD BANK
Washington, D.C.

Contents

About the Authors

Catherine Aubert

Catherine Aubert joined Société Générale in 1999 as an Insurance Specialist. In 2006, she moved to the Corporate & Investment Banking Division of Société Générale, where she heads the Trade Credit & Political Risks Insurance Department. Prior to joining Société Générale, Ms. Aubert spent ten years with Group Paribas in various positions and three years as a Financial Institutions Development Manager with an insurance broker (now known as Marsh McLennan).

Ms. Aubert graduated from EDHEC Management School and has a Master in Communication from CELSA (Paris Sorbonne University).

Tony George

Tony George is a partner with Ince & Co. Mr. George has been involved in almost all of the political risk insurance claims in the London Market which have required legal input over the last 35 years, acting for insurers, brokers, insureds or their financing banks. He has also helped develop political and credit risk insurance products. Mr. George has been involved in several hundred claims in over 80 countries—from Afghanistan to Zimbabwe. He is also a frequent speaker and writer on the subject.

Izumi Kobayashi

Izumi Kobayashi joined the Multilateral Investment Guarantee Agency (MIGA) as Executive Vice President on November 24, 2008.

Ms. Kobayashi came to MIGA from Merrill Lynch in Tokyo, where she was President and Representative Director. She joined Merrill Lynch in 1985 to work on the derivatives markets, and subsequently held a number of high-level global leadership roles, including serving as Director of Operations and Chief Administrative Officer. As President, Ms. Kobayashi successfully developed the company's business in global financial services and its client franchise, working with international teams ranging in size from 10 people to over 1,000.

A graduate of Seikei University in Japan, Ms. Kobayashi was featured in the October 2005 edition of the Wall Street Journal's "50 Women to Watch," and in 2004 she received the following award from Veuve Clicquot, "The Business Woman of the Year." She is active in promoting opportunities for women and young professionals in the workplace and is a board member of *Keizai Doyukai*, the Japanese association of corporate executives.

Sabine Konrad

Dr. Sabine Konrad is a German *Rechtsanwältin*. Her principal area of practice is international dispute resolution, in particular international arbitration and public international law. She regularly advises investors and governments in matters of investment protection. Dr. Konrad also sits as arbitrator.

In 2007, Dr. Konrad was designated by the Government of the Federal Republic of Germany to the Panel of Arbitrators of the World Bank's International Centre for Settlement of Investment Disputes (ICSID). In 2005, she was closely involved in setting up the Frankfurt International Arbitration Center, which serves as a cooperation facility of ICSID for investment treaty arbitrations in Germany. Dr. Konrad is the founder of the Frankfurt Investment Arbitration Moot.

Dr. Konrad earned a diploma from the University of London, and an LL.M. Eur. from Ludwig-Maximilians-University in Munich. She received a J.D. from the University of Passau, Germany.

Julie Martin

Julie Martin, a Senior Vice President in the Political Risk Practice of Marsh USA, is based in Washington, DC. She is responsible for development and management of the political risk business in the Mid-Atlantic and South regions.

Ms. Martin's work in political risk includes program structure, exposure analysis, insurance placement, and claims advisory for a variety of industries. These included large complex mining and infrastructure transactions, multicountry placements, supplier credit and bank financing arrangements, and capital market securitizations. Ms. Martin has worked extensively with both public and private political risk underwriters in manuscripting policy wording to address complex risks and exposures.

Ms. Martin joined Marsh in 2001 after 20 years of experience in the political risk business at the Overseas Private Investment Corporation (OPIC), the U.S. government agency charged with promoting U.S. investment in emerging markets. At OPIC, Ms. Martin served in a variety of positions, including chief underwriter and head of the political risk insurance department. She was responsible for many of the initiatives by OPIC in the political risk area including development of programs for institutional lenders and the capital markets. During this time, Ms. Martin underwrote or managed the issuance of several hundred political risk policies for both large and small businesses in all parts of the emerging markets and developing world across many lines of industry and services.

Ms. Martin received a B.G.S. in International Relations from Texas Tech University, an M.S. in Foreign Service from Georgetown University, and an M.B.A. in Finance from George Washington University.

Robert C. O'Sullivan

Robert C. O'Sullivan is Acting Deputy General Counsel and Associate General Counsel for Insurance and Claims of the Overseas Private Investment Corporation (OPIC). He advises the Vice President and General Counsel on a variety of legal and policy issues, assists in management of the Office of Legal Affairs, provides legal advice to the Insurance Department on contract origination and development of new products, and handles claims arising from OPIC's political risk insurance program, managing OPIC's dealings with the insured investor, other U.S. government agencies, and the foreign government involved. He has also negotiated a number of the intergovernmental agreements under which OPIC operates around the world, most recently, a replacement agreement with Indonesia.

Mr. O'Sullivan has been an adjunct professor at Georgetown University Law Center and American University's Washington College of Law. He is also a frequent speaker at OPIC's internal training programs and client conferences and at international law and investment meetings outside of OPIC. Prior to joining OPIC's legal staff in 1981, Mr. O'Sullivan was an associate in the Washington office of Sutherland, Asbill & Brennan.

Anne Marie Thurber

Anne Marie Thurber joined Zurich Emerging Markets Solutions in July 1999 and in 2008 was named to Senior Vice President and Managing Director, Credit and Political Risk. She is based in Washington, DC. Prior to joining Zurich, Ms. Thurber began her underwriting career in 1992 and served as regional manager for Latin America and the Caribbean at the Multilateral Investment Guarantee Agency (MIGA), as well as regional manager for Latin America and the former Soviet Union regions at the Overseas Private Investment Corporation (OPIC). Before joining OPIC, Ms. Thurber worked in the reinsurance and manufacturing sectors.

Ms. Thurber holds a B.S. from Louisiana State University, an M.B.A. from Tulane University, and an M.A. from the Johns Hopkins University School of Advanced International Studies (SAIS).

Gerald T. West

Gerald T. West is currently an Adjunct Professor of International Business Diplomacy at Georgetown University. Retiring from the Multilateral Investment Guarantee Agency (MIGA) in mid-2006, he had held five different positions in four different MIGA departments, including Senior Advisor, Guarantees; Director of Evaluation; Director of Policy and the Environment; and Claims Administrator. Prior to serving at MIGA for 15 years, he held a variety of positions at the Overseas Private Investment Corporation (OPIC), including ten years as the Vice President of Development and Chairman of the Investment Committee.

For nine years, Dr. West held a variety of research and administrative positions at the Foreign Policy Research Institute where he conducted research on a wide range of international political and economic issues. This research involved both empirical, statistical, and policy analyses. He was the chief methodologist on a variety of future studies for several U.S. Government agencies.

From 1983 to 1995 and again from 2003 to the present, Dr. West has served as an Adjunct Professor in the Landegger International Business Diplomacy Program at Georgetown University. His primary course offering has been "International Political Risk Assessment and Management." Over the last 30 years, he has lectured, consulted, and published widely on corporate political risk assessment and management. His most recent books included coediting the papers from two MIGA-Georgetown Symposia on International Political Risk Management.

Dr. West received his Ph.D. in International Politics from the Wharton School of the University of Pennsylvania.

David Wright

David Wright is the Chief Underwriting Officer for the London/European division of CV Starr's Political & Financial Risk unit. He has 25 years of experience in the insurance industry, principally in political risk. The first half of his career was in the broking sector, moving to underwriting in 1998 when he joined XL Capital's Lloyd's of London operation. He eventually became XL Insurance's Global Practice Leader for War & Political Risks. He joined Starr in 2008 to establish a new Political & Financial risk operation.

CHAPTER 1

Introduction

Izumi Kobayashi

It is a pleasure for me to introduce *Old Risks-New Solutions, or Is It the Other Way Around?*, the sixth volume in the International Political Risk Management Series, and now a World Bank Studies publication. The chapters that follow represent recent viewpoints on political risk management issues, which were presented at the Seventh Biannual MIGA-Georgetown Symposium. The Symposium was hosted by the Multilateral Investment Guarantee Agency and Georgetown University on October 28, 2010.

Events like the Multilateral Investment Guarantee Agency (MIGA)-Georgetown Symposium demonstrate that there is much to be learned through the sharing of experiences and thinking together about the critical issues that confront our industry as well as new products and ideas.

External Environment

In November 2008, the time of the last symposium, our attention was focused on unfolding of the financial crisis. Only two months had passed since the collapse of Lehman Brothers, yet we had already witnessed the beginning of steep decline in foreign direct investment flows not only to the developing countries but all over the world. Investment projects were frozen or cancelled as available credit contracted or disappeared altogether. As new details emerged, it became increasingly unclear just how bad and how far reaching the financial crisis would become.

In 2010, from MIGA's point of view, there were signs that foreign direct investment (FDI) was beginning to recover. Although the credit environment was still tight, with many banks were still holding on their capital as opposed to extending credit, the appetite for investment was beginning grow stronger. However, investors still faced challenges. Established investors felt that their balance sheet was strong enough to warrant the risk of not ensuring the investment while smaller investors were often facing a higher probability of difficulty after the start of project. Many small investors lacked the expertise to properly manage the political risk while fierce competition in large markets forces others to look to less competitive but risky markets. On the other hand, as margins became thinner, investors needed ask themselves if the benefit of political risk insurance (PRI) outweighed the cost.

Investors also faced new challenges involving regulatory systems. For example, the initial discussions on Basel III presented uncertainty regarding the implications of the new system on capital requirements and to what extent if any investors would be able to benefit from using PRI. This is particularly relevant for the financing of investment projects whereas financing agents have looked to PRI to provide relief to capital and provisioning requirement.

In respect to the financial crisis, MIGA's primary source of new business during 2009 was in the financial sector in Eastern and Central Europe and Central Asia so called the Europe and Central Asia region. This region was most affected and in need of financial and capital injections. Investments in other sectors and regions declined dramatically during this period.

During the latter half of 2009 and 2010, MIGA witnessed an increase in both the sectoral and regional diversity of new investment. However, investors were becoming much more selective in which project that they were willing to undertake. At the same time, it was noted that when investors did focus resources on a particular project, the probability of execution became very high.

Since the end of 2010, the world has witnessed the Arab Spring, and a series of regime changes in the Middle East and North Africa (MENA) region. Beginning with Tunisia, and followed by the Arab Republic of Egypt and Libya, long-standing governments fell to the forces of popular discontent and a strong desire for change. MIGA has supported investments in each of these countries subsequent to the change of power, and continues to consider the region as a strategic priority for new investments.

One of our key questions we are faced with is how the investment market has changed as a result of the financial crisis—how do current trends differ from the FDI boom that preceded the crisis? How have the money flows changed in terms of volume and how have they been flowing? How recovery in the one country affects its neighbors? From a business point of view, one of the challenges is knowing which country will emerge as the growth engine for that region.

The political risk appetite for investors is changing. MIGA's exposure concentration has shifted over time from Brazil to Europe and Central Asia region, and now it's moving into other regions. PRI can be viewed as an indicator of economic and market growth and change. Trends show an increase in outbound investments from the middle income countries like Brazil, Turkey, China as well as some of the more advanced African countries. MIGA has witnessed a dramatic shift away from a concentration of exposure in the financial sector and into infrastructure, energy and power projects.

Developments in Political Risk Management

Since the last symposium, there have been a number of important changes in MIGA. Most noticeably and recently, The Agency was able to enact a number of changes to our convention. MIGA can now guarantee stand-alone debt and existing investment projects. Whereas the PRI market has been issuing such insurance for many years, these new covers represent an important step toward keeping pace with market development and investor demand. Unlike private market insurers and expert credit agencies, MIGA is very restricted in what it is able to do by its' convention and international treaty with 175 signatories. MIGA also added nonhonoring of sovereign international obligations to its four traditional covers last year.

MIGA opened a new Asian hub in Singapore with underwriters in Hong Kong SAR, China and business development staff in Beijing and Tokyo. This hub aims to capitalize on Asian emerging as a new center of outbound investment growth. We have seen a growing base of investors in China as well as other Asian countries looking to go into the challenging market. MIGA also opened a business development office in Paris, which will focus on new business opportunities in Europe as well as the Middle East and North Africa. We view both of these hubs as providing an excellent opportunity for MIGA to support the economic growth of low-income countries through providing the support to South-South investments. Providing PRI for outbound investment from the rich and other middle-income countries has become more important as the level of FDI growth from these countries has increased.

CHAPTER 2

Changing Perspectives of Risk in the Aftermath of the Financial Crisis: A London Political Risk Insurer's View

David Wright

With the relative calm of the current global economic situation as the backdrop to this latest Multilateral Investment Guarantee Agency (MIGA)-Georgetown symposium, it is in some ways hard to believe the very different situation and mood that existed at the time of the last event here only two years ago. In October 2008, with the collapse of Lehman Brothers only a month old and the financial markets in the grip of a vicious downward spiral, to picture a world on the very edge of the abyss did not seem overly dramatic. Early impressions were that the world had likely changed forever and that the risk dynamics in which the political risk insurance industry operated were moving along lines not seen before. So, barely 25 months after the maelstrom, what happened in the meantime, and where are we now? This chapter gives the perspective of a London-based private market political risk insurer, active in the following fields:

- Investment insurance (protecting investments and assets against expropriatory acts, currency inconvertibility, and physical damage from war or terrorism)
- Contract frustration (frustration of contracts for the sale or purchase of goods or services, or the financing of these, because of government actions, including nonpayment and nondelivery)
- Structured trade credit (contract frustration but because of the actions or inactions by private-status obligors).

What has been seen on the other side of the Atlantic may be a proxy for the global political risk industry in terms of claims, relative demand for other products, insurer capabilities and appetite, and market conditions.

Although Starr Political and Financial Risk was in start-up mode in 2008, the company witnessed the chaotic events of that September and onward at close hand. The political risk market had enjoyed a relatively benign time in the preceding years: although the combined catastrophe events of September 11, 2001, and the Argentine crisis of 2001 had not been forgotten and their legacy was still being felt, the insurance market in the intervening years had enjoyed pretty good fortune, albeit with the punctuation of some specific country and obligor events.

In terms of the makeup of the private market, spending a couple of minutes looking at the macro changes in market products and priorities is helpful to set the scene: some 15 years before the crisis, Lloyd's political risk was dominated by investment and asset confiscation–type coverages. Premiums from this subclass were twice that of contract frustration and trade credit combined. By 2001, investment and asset insurance was about equal in premium terms to that of contract frustration and trade credit. In 2008, that pendulum had swung farther, and investment and asset premiums were only a quarter of the combined total for contract frustration and trade credit. Similarly, Xchanging Claims Services, the body that administers and processes Lloyd's underwriters' claims, reports that from 1996 to 2008, almost 50 percent of the market's payments were in respect of investment and asset losses. That was the backdrop. So what happened in the past two years?

Insurers produce what they call realistic disaster scenarios, in which they model theoretical major loss events with which to test robustness of aggregation limitations, reinsurance purchasing strategy, and capital allocation. These disaster scenarios vary from class to class: aviation insurers might worry about collision between two airliners over a major city, and energy underwriters might concern themselves with a high number of hurricanes in the Gulf of Mexico. For political risk insurers, with risk factors and dynamics that constantly change, realistic disaster scenarios are a mixture of country, regional, sectoral, and event scenarios, and these evolve as politico-economic factors evolve. Nobody thought of the following scenario, however: a global economic crisis, affecting pretty much all countries, all sectors, and all at once. No, that was just too fantastic a proposition.

It seemed at the time that the consequences of an effective cessation of finance would be worryingly far-reaching: no country or industry seemed definitely safe. Political risk insurers are used to answering questions from their management about exposures to individual country events, but no comfort could seemingly be given to management two years ago on where losses would end up. That said, and with reference to realistic disaster scenarios, the older hands in the market pointed to previous loss events where actual losses were usually a small percentage of maximum exposure. And so it turned out. Even though insurers were deluged with notices of events of default from the banks that represent an increasingly large part of the collective client base, Armageddon did not happen. For all political risk insurers, and particularly those with structured trade credit operations, the end of 2008 and a good part of 2009 were dominated by restructurings and workouts. Some situations were beyond salvation, but where insurers were willing to work with their borrowers, obligor default claims were minimized. For investment and asset insurance, putting to one side the relatively special situations in left-leaning Latin America in particular, claims that might have been foreseen in countries experiencing severe economic difficulties have not materialized. Demonstrating the inherent resilience in the sectors insured (investment and trade for the most part), one can now say that the market and its clients did a stellar job of containment.

One can take the Lloyd's market situation as a proxy for private market experience. To date, Lloyd's has paid out claims totaling some US$500 million. Although a high number by anyone's reckoning, and in recognition that this crisis has perhaps not yet run its course, interestingly the claims paid over the past two years were only 275 percent of the annual average payout of the previous decade. Again, this figure is a large jump, but when compared to how things might have been and against the background of an unprecedented global crisis, it looks like a good result. The private market has paid out punctually, and clients and brokers alike have indicated that they are delighted with how the products have performed.

So what were the claims that have been incurred? Of the claims in London, the bulk seem to have come from four main sources:

- Ukraine (banks)
- Kazakhstan (banks)
- Bahrain (banks)
- Brazil (agriculture).

The balance of the claims are from one-off situations in various locations, but the bulk of the problems are as noted above. By way of the main contrast with the last major loss event, that of Argentina in 2001 onward, in which most of the claims were investment related, the statistics here are very different. For 2009–10, fewer than 10 percent of the total paid claims were made up of investment losses. The main component was by far trade credit, accounting for two-thirds of the payouts. The next highest subclass was contract frustration, at just over 20 percent, so obligor default products accounted for almost 90 percent of the losses. Clearly, the loss activity centers on these two products, which says a lot about where the political risk market has gone.

During the crisis, through the fog of fear that pretty much engulfed all industries, the political risk insurance industry felt that risk aversion would be a predominant factor going forward. Again going back to the parallel of 2001, in this case September 11, the cliché of the terrorism market was that suddenly chicken farmers in Idaho felt they neededto buy coverage: in the absence of knowing just how widespread the new peril would be, a rush to insure occurred. Going back to 2008, again in the absence of knowing what the future would hold, most insurers in the political risk sector expected that demand for its product would rocket, irrespective of supply-side dynamics. Looking back, one can probably say with truth that what insurers saw in late 2008 and early 2009 was an increase in the range of countries for which insureds inquired and, in the deleveraging panic, there was some evidence of banks selling down existing positions. However, a few points should be made clear:

- Demand to sell down was pretty much exclusively in obligor default products.
- New business was very limited and was concentrated very much on the trade side (people still needed fuel and food): new investments, however, were rare.
- Consequently, demand for investment and asset insurance was limited. The most meaningful "new" investment and asset insurance were seen related to shareholder loans to foreign-owned banks in emerging markets that desperately needed liquidity, where the crisis meant that borrowing locally was very difficult.
- Demand for political risk insurance products was definitely enhanced by banks' inability to retain risk on the level of individual inability to hold as much as previously, plus the collapse of sharing risk with other banks through the suspension of the syndication market.

Thus, the first nine months after the crisis saw investment fall off a cliff, and world trade significantly diminished. What transactions were seen did indeed lead to an increase in diversification by country and obligor, but new deals were few and far between and closure pace was glacial. Since that time, the past year has seen a gradual (and tentative) return of confidence. World trade has picked up again, and signs are present of a recovery of sorts. However, in what has happened recently, the following points apply:

- The insurance inquiries received reflect only gradually returning confidence, and growth has been mainly in the "essentials": supply of energy, food, and finance.
- Virtually no infrastructure inquiries have been seen. Investment insurance interest has been in areas such as finance and natural resources.
- Although banks retain a degree of risk aversion, confidence has returned here, too, and the syndication market is regaining its strength.
- Finally, and still on the subject of banks, one of the prevalent themes of the past year has been cost of funds: banks have to pay more for their own borrowings, and this limits what they are prepared to pay on insurance.

As regards insurers, the past two years have unquestionably provided the biggest challenge to the market since its formation some 40 years ago. As mentioned earlier, the time after the financial crisis brought waves of potential claims and notifications of events of default across collective portfolios, causing most agencies to focus firmly upon dealing with existing problems rather than looking for new business opportunities. Many were occupied with restructurings and workouts pretty much full time in the year after September 2008. A claims manager of one leading broking house in this area confirmed that they had seen more new advices of potential or actual clams in one month than they had seen in the previous three years. However, the volume of new advices began to abate, and although some new circumstances come in from time to time, a feeling now exists that, barring a fresh return to the turmoil, that phase of the crisis at least is over. Thus, the business has moved on from where it was two years ago, when insurers across the board were looking only half-heartedly at new opportunities and were quite content to put income and growth targets on the back burner. The situation definitely began to ease in the second half of 2009, and insurers, like their clients, began to look more to the future and to refocus upon new business rather than problem situations.

What has happened to overall political risk insurance market capacity over the past two years? The answer seems to be precious little. One market broker estimates that collective insurer capacity is almost identical to that precrisis. Perhaps a little less is available for large credit deals than before because, in view of the preponderance of losses in that subclass, individual agencies are writing more conservative lines. One of the presumed drivers for capacity contraction was the 2010 reinsurance renewal: reinsurers were expected to withdraw or scale back from credit in particular. In reality, that never happened. Whether because of a desire to achieve payback for past losses or whether because of the relative attraction of political risk compared with the softening property and casualty markets, capacity remained largely unscathed. Similarly, the 2011 renewal is expected to be kind to cedants.

What of policy terms and pricing? A distinction can be drawn between the obligor default products (contract frustration and trade credit), on the one hand, and the investment and asset confiscation product suite, on the other. For the former, insurance market offerings have really mirrored the situation in financial markets. In late 2008 and early 2009, in response to evaporating liquidity and all-pervading risk aversion, margins (and therefore premiums) rocketed, and the emerging-market bond indexes spiked spectacularly. Similarly, structures became very conservative, and substantial emerging-market borrowers who had largely been able to dictate their own debt structures before were now corralled into very short-term, heavily structured transactions. Since then, a gradual retreat has occurred, and now risk margins on obligor default insurances are almost exactly where they were precrisis. However, these margins are still probably twice what they were at the start of the credit crunch in 2007. In addition, structures remain far superior, and these are relaxing much more slowly than rates. With respect to investment and asset insurances, one can truthfully say that the same volatility did not occur. Rates have remained fairly constant and, although one can argue that the expropriation risk is better or worse in times of economic crisis (worse because governments may resort to emergency measures that harm investment, or better because the governments will not want to discourage what little investment exists), the net result seems to be rates that did not leap upward and are now level or slightly down.

Following are some thoughts on the lessons that can be drawn from the "crisis experience," both for the political risk product range as a whole and specifically for the investment insurance subclass.

First, the crisis has proven beyond any doubt at all that the political risk insurance product works. The value of the checks cut by Lloyd's, as only one market participant, has been mentioned, and these are very significant numbers. A few gray areas existed in the political risks claims activity following the 2001 Argentine experience, but the 2008 financial crisis has provided incontrovertible evidence that these insurance products work.

Second, the shift in the makeup of the political risk market, from confiscation-type perils and exchange transfer and toward obligor default products, has continued. Even though investment will pick up, this division of emphasis will probably continue and can be expected to define insurers' product offerings for the foreseeable future.

Third, although the cost of the exercise was on the high side, the learning experience was meaningful. As previously mentioned, for insureds and their brokers political risk insurance really works. Some more occasional purchasers of these insurance products, precrisis, explained that the one doubt they had about insurance was how it would actually perform when needed. They have had that experience now, and even though other risk mitigants will unquestionably come back into play, one hopes insureds will not forget those who were there to stand up and be counted during the darkest of days. From the insurers' perspective, many lessons were learned and questions posed, in large measure the same ones as applied to the policyholders. Whether it was the way security could be enforced in practice as distinct from in theory, or the prioritization of trade debt over other forms, insureds are now somewhat wiser. However, with specific reference to trade debt, the evidence of the logic of insuring trade and investment is manifest in the results of insurers in these sectors compared with those in other financial sectors. On a micro level, insurers have responded in approach in the same ways as their insureds: with more caution and certainly with more emphasis on risk structures. In common with previous crises, though, one factor has persisted: who you insure is as important, if not more important, than what or where you insure. Policyholders who are willing to work with insurers to resolve problems and who treat insurance as a backstop when all loss-mitigation efforts have been exhausted—and not a put option— are the clients that are still needed. Such a base of insureds has been an important factor in the market's results from the crisis.

Finally, investment insurance was never a universal tool, nor should one expect it to be. Investors do not always buy political risk insurance for a number of reasons:

- They are often confident in their own risk management capabilities as an alternative means of dealing with the risks. Significantly, in MIGA's study *World Investment and Political Risk 2009* (MIGA 2010), of the investors questioned on their overall political risk assessment in anticipating new political risks, implementing existing political risk strategies, and evaluating new political risk strategies, over 65 percent felt they rated good to excellent.
- Similarly, respondents believe other means of mitigating risk can be used, such as dialogue with government and coventuring with respected local partners.
- Not all investors believe their industries are risky enough to warrant buying political risk insurance. As mentioned previously, the bulk of the inquiries still seems to lie in relatively high-profile industries such as the natural resource sectors.
- An appetite for risk still exists outside the insurance industry, and one should not forget or be concerned at this. Equity investors realize that risk and return are interlinked and are often happy to run this risk. From a debt perspective, confidence is returning to the banking markets, and with particular reference to the obligor default products, insurers are definitely seeing that the syndication market is back. This market provides an alternative to political risk insurances.
- Alternatives often exist. For obligor default products, credit default swaps are available on a certain number of names, the bank syndication market (as mentioned earlier) is active, and self-insurance is always a possibility. Similarly, for investment insurers, self-insurance is an ever-present feature. However, as the structured trade credit market expands, lenders who might previously have covered an emerging market project against political-only perils can often now buy an obligor-default policy that wraps in all elements of the risk.
- Cost is, was, and always will be a factor. At the symposium in 2004, Clive Tobin, the chief executive officer at XL, drew attention to the fact that even though risk awareness was heightened following September 11, 2001, and the Argentine experience, many companies' budgets for insurance were completely consumed by the much more expensive traditional property and casualty coverages. Similarly, even though risk awareness concerns are heightened now, in the current climate of scare liquidity and recession, money is not always available for insurance that is still a discretionary purchase in many cases.
- One should not forget that not all emerging markets were equally affected by the crisis. The aforementioned MIGA (2010) study notes that many countries in Latin America and Asia have performed rather well during the crisis, and investors are generally far more sanguine about countries here than they are about some of those in the Euro Area.

- Finally, one must not forget that investment has been minimal. When this returns, as it undoubtedly will, investment insurance will have a part to play. Because of the nature of the industry, many investors in infrastructure will not invest without insurance. Similarly, many private market insurers in such sectors will provide coverage only alongside public insurers.

To end, the past two years have been a period like no other for the political risk insurance industry. It appears to have weathered the storm and with a combination of hard work, courage, flexibility, and good policyholders reached a stage where the situation in October 2010 is unequivocally better than could have been foreseen at the time of the last symposium. Political risk insurance products still have a major part to play, and although obligor default products are now very much at the forefront, investment insurance will continue to be more important than it recently has been as investment becomes more in evidence.

CHAPTER 3

OPIC's Shadow Claims History

Robert C. O'Sullivan

The final claims determinations (claims paid and denied) by the Overseas Private Investment Corporation (OPIC) are publicly available, and a cumulative claims history is published annually. As of September 30, 2010, OPIC paid 290 claims totaling US$969.8 million and denied 28 claims, 14 of which were submitted to arbitration.

At the 2004 International Political Risk Management symposium hosted by the Multilateral Investment Guarantee Agency (MIGA) and Georgetown University on November 12, I presented a paper titled "Learning from OPIC's Experience with Claims and Arbitration" that included a discussion of what can be learned from "near claims."

This chapter expands on what can be learned from claims matters that never received a final determination and thus that remain in the "shadows," as opposed to the final claim determinations that OPIC makes publicly available. Those *shadow claims* include (a) situations that OPIC monitored when multiple claims seemed likely because of serious country issues, (b) specific projects for which the investor sent OPIC a notice of potential claim but made no claim, (c) investment disputes in which the insured investor requested an OPIC intervention (advocacy), and (d) claims that were filed but were withdrawn before a decision was made.

Overview of the Data

Information regarding shadow claims is not as complete or as uniform as that for decided claims, but OPIC has enough data on approximately 100 shadow claims to offer overall generalizations and to present some specific case studies. Infrastructure projects account for almost one-third of the total claims, with power projects taking the lead (table 3.1). Thus, adding oil and gas projects (12) and mining projects (5) to infrastructure projects would account for almost half of those claims (47). The further addition of projects involving land use rights—hotel and real estate (8) and agribusiness (5)—would account for 60 percent of the shadow claims. By adding contractors and exporters, always a source of disputes, one can account for nearly two-thirds of the total.

Table 3.1 Shadow Claims within Sectors

Sector	Number of claims
Infrastructure	
Power	17
Telecommunications	8
Water	3
Transport	2
Total Infrastructure	30
Selected others	
Oil and gas	12
Hotel and real estate	8
Contractor and exporter	7
Mining	5
Agribusiness	5

Source: World Bank data.

Analysis of the Data

Around 30–40 years ago, the conventional underwriting analysis of the data would have found that the high incidence of infrastructure claims can be explained by the government's natural role in providing essential services and that the high incidence of natural resource and land use claims can be explained by its desire to protect the national patrimony.

Those considerations certainly remain a factor, but a complication has arisen in the past 20 years or so, which is the time period to which almost all the shadow claims relate. In that period, there has been a dramatic increase in the number of infrastructure projects that have been financed by foreign private investment on terms that were intended to improve or expand the availability of essential services while generating a profit for the investors.

Once the services are in place, or nearly in place, many factors can upset the assumptions on which the investor's projections were based. The investor's expectation of a profit may run up against the expectation of the public that such services ought to be provided at no cost or at subsidized prices as "social rights"—an expectation that the government may encourage by legislation or by the lack of it. The investor's financial projections may not have accounted for the reality that utility bills are uncollectible as a practical matter or are avoidable by easy theft of services. The investor's market projections may have been unduly optimistic, and filing a political risk insurance claim may become an exit strategy.

The host country's government may experience an economic crisis that undoes everyone's assumptions, and its crisis management strategy may include repudiating investment agreements that it can no longer afford. The situation is further complicated if the investment was made in conjunction with the privatization of a government-owned service provider, thereby putting the foreign private investor in conflict with public employee unions and other interest groups. Yet another complication is that so many of these projects were undertaken in emerging-market economies, where legal systems were in flux, that there was a lack of experience with private investment and pricing mechanisms, and the profit motive was initially suspect.

Relationship of Shadow Claims History to Paid Claims History

OPIC's history of shadow claims is dominated by potential expropriation claims. In that respect, it somewhat reflects OPIC's published claims history of the past 20 years: the incidence of payment of expropriation claims has increased, and they cannot all be avoided, even with timely notice and intervention. Since 1971, expropriation claims paid by OPIC account for 23 percent of total claims paid, whereas in the past 20 years, they account for 38 percent of the total.

However, the larger shift in the character of claims paid is away from inconvertibility and toward political violence, and that shift is not reflected in the shadow claims history. Overall, inconvertibility claims account for 60 percent of the total claims paid but only 7 percent of claims paid in the past 20 years, whereas political violence claims account for 18 percent of the overall total but 55 percent of the claims paid in the past 20 years. Except for countrywide monitoring in a period of heightened risk, one would not expect political violence claims to be part of the shadow claims history, because the events of recovery so often occur without notice and because neither the investor nor the insurer can prevent them or reverse their consequences, as might occur in the case of an investment dispute.

The substance of many expropriation claims that OPIC paid during this period reflects the same type of conflicts that characterize the shadow claims, namely, the conflicts that can arise when projects that once would have been undertaken by governments (with their own funds or with bilateral or multilateral assistance) are instead structured as public-private partnerships, with (a) lenders who expect to be repaid on time at market rates of interest, (b) contractors who expect to be paid for services rendered, and (c) equity investors who seek a return on their investment.

The Alliant TechSystems claims in Belarus (1997) and Ukraine (1999) were related to projects to recycle obsolete munitions by selling the components, particularly metals, on world markets. Using a foreign contractor so close to the defense sector may have been part of the problem, even though foreign investment in defense conversion was thought to be in the common interest. The D. Joseph Companies claim in Jamaica (1999) arose from an investment agreement that was made when the country was a closed economy and that was no longer viable under free market conditions. The MidAmerican claim in Indonesia (2000), several Dabhol Power Company–related claims in India (2003/04), and the Bank of America and AES Corporation claims in Colombia (2004) arose from power projects. The SAIC (Science Applications International Corporation) claim in the República Bolivariana de Venezuela (2004) was based on the disputed termination of a joint venture that provided information technology to the government-owned oil company. The Ponderosa claim in Argentina (2005) was based on the government's repudiation of a licensing agreement as a result of emergency measures taken to deal with an economic crisis. The Uniworld Holdings Ltd. claim in Serbia (2008) arose from the wrongful calling of a performance bond that was posted in connection with the privatization of tourism facilities.

The decision documents on all these claims are available on OPIC's website (http://www.opic.gov), as is OPIC's cumulative insurance claims history.

Monitored Claims

Monitoring potential claim situations amounts to proactive self-education, preparation, and above-average client contact in anticipation of foreseeable claims. OPIC has monitored specific projects and also its entire country portfolio. For example, during the Argentine debt crisis (2001), it reviewed all Argentine projects for which it had inconvertibility exposure, analyzed foreign exchange regulations and their potential effect on each project, and updated its analyses regularly. When exchange controls were imposed in Venezuela in February 2003, OPIC took the additional measure of retaining local counsel and organized seminars involving the investors and the new regulator, the Commission for the Administration of Currency Exchange (Comisión de Administración de Divisas, or CADIVI), to ensure better understanding of the regulations and CADIVI application procedures. Ultimately, OPIC paid no inconvertibility claims in Argentina, paid one in Venezuela, and continues to monitor the situation in Venezuela.

Notice of Potential Claims

OPIC insurance contracts contain the typical requirement that the insured notify the insurer of potential claims. Failure to give timely notice may justify denial of a claim, and thus, some investors give notice as a protective measure even when the likelihood of a claim is remote. Early notice and informative updates facilitate advocacy efforts that may avert a claim. Claims for which the investor gave notice solely as a protective matter may simply lapse.

Problems Solved by Others

Other claims do not simply lapse but are resolved without intervention by the insurer. Some disputes are resolved by the parties directly involved without assistance from others, and some are resolved by unforeseen third parties. In one case, purchasers of the output of a mine that was shut down as the result of an investment dispute brought pressure to reopen the mine. In another case, OPIC-equivalent agencies, acting independently and in their own interest, solved OPIC's problem as well as their own. In yet another case, European and Arab sources financed reconstruction of a power plant, thereby averting OPIC's payment on a substantial political violence claim.

Advocacy

Advocacy refers to intervention by the insurer (and perhaps others) at an appropriate level to produce a favorable outcome to an investment dispute (and perhaps avert a claim). Advocacy may be bilateral or multilateral (or at least multiparty). Examples include intervention by senior OPIC officials visiting the project country to obtain release of a performance bond, intervention by the U.S. embassy to persuade the foreign government to adhere to the agreed dispute resolution procedures, and intervention by the U.S. consulate with local officials to resolve issues relating to a local public-private partnership. In cooperation with other U.S. government agencies, OPIC can engage in advocacy in conjunction with bilateral or multilateral meetings on more general subjects, raising the investor's complaint to a higher level and putting it in context. Reminding visiting foreign government officials on an investment promotion campaign that treating existing investors fairly ought to be their first step and that a pending dispute has attention can be effective. When a project's host country government has taken action that affects foreign investors of several nations, OPIC can coordinate with parallel agencies of the other countries. For example, for an issue affecting all projects that rely on a particular financial structure, many public and private lenders and insurers will have an interest in resolving it.

"Advocacy Plus"

In some cases, OPIC has gone beyond writing letters and arranging meetings at appropriate levels; it has supported the dispute resolution process with its own insurance or financing. For example, OPIC resolved disputes relating to two oil and gas concessions in a Central American country by financing the expenses of consultative meetings with the local communities that led to new concession agreements. The existing agreements had been challenged in a local court for failure to consult the local communities, and an injunction had been issued for failure to hold the meetings. However, the affected community-level organizations had no funding to attend a meeting in the capital to consider whether to grant approval. An issue existed whether consultation was required, and the local communities actually appeared to welcome the projects, but all parties put those issues aside and concentrated on satisfying the formality that was required by the court order. OPIC insisted on a clear agreement that it was providing funding for travel and other out-of-pocket expenses of the process, without regard to the outcome. In addition, there was a tight budget and strict accounting for the expenditures, which were insignificant in relation to the potential claims. Ultimately, the investors and local communities approved new, mutually acceptable concession agreements.

In another case, OPIC was a project lender as well an insurer and, as lender, facilitated a buyout of an investor that led to withdrawal of the insurance claim. In other cases, OPIC used its loan guaranty authority to permit the host country government to borrow that government's share of a claim settlement with the insured and used the local currency salvage provisions of its intergovernmental agreement to permit the host country government to pay part of the government's settlement in local currency while compensating the investor in dollars.

Pitfalls of Advocacy

Insurers, especially public sector insurers, emphasize the special role that they can play in dispute resolution, and each of them has its success stories. However, advocacy has its pitfalls. In general, the problem is that, in the event of failure, the investor may attempt to portray the advocacy effort as tantamount to a provisional claim determination in the investor's favor, although the insurer undertook the advocacy effort without completing its normal, rigorous claims procedures.

The specific possibilities include backing an investor who is in the wrong, acting on the basis of invalid assumptions about local law, becoming allied with an unreasonable or uncooperative partner, and, in the worst case, being accused of bad faith for having done everything possible to avoid facing up to an "obviously" valid claim.

Withdrawn Claims

The nearest of near claims is one in which a completed application for compensation has been submitted but is later withdrawn. The most common situation is an inconvertibility claim for which the investor obtains foreign exchange through the normal channel while a political risk claim is pending. The investor has received foreign exchange, no longer holds the local currency, and wants to preserve insurance capacity for the future. In addition, the undisputed effect of a contract provision may appear only during the insurer's processing of an application for compensation. For example, if the contract contains a deductible, its effect may not appear until the insurer determines the amount of compensation that would be payable without a deductible.

Finally, in the case of a claim that is about to be denied, OPIC's practice is to allow the insured to review the draft determination and offer comments. The procedure is intended to ensure that a final determination is made on the basis of all the information that the insured considers relevant and that OPIC has given proper consideration to the investor's position on the key issues. In a recent case, the investor withdrew its claim instead.

Conclusion

OPIC's published record of claim determinations has its own limitations and distortions, described in the earlier chapter (O'Sullivan 2004). OPIC's experience is not a general measure of the level of political risk. On the one hand, it may not have been active in problem countries or may not have supported the categories of projects that were most likely to encounter problems, which would tend to understate country risk. On the other hand, multiple claims arising from the same project could overstate country risk.

The shadow claims history suffers from both gaps in data and inconsistent data that have become more apparent than ever in the writing and revision of this chapter. For example, it would be interesting to know OPIC's potential liability for each of the shadow claims, and it would be helpful to have a cumulative shadow claims history organized by year to parallel the cumulative history of claims paid. Unfortunately, those issues were not raised during organization of the data that was available. Nevertheless, trying to construct OPIC's shadow claims history has been a useful project. Insurers that may have relatively infrequent experience with claims paid but make extensive use of reinsurance probably have systematic reports from which to construct their own shadow claims histories. Near claims—shadow claims—are more than near misses to the balance sheet; they are learning experiences for insurer and insured alike.

CHAPTER 4

Claims and Recoveries in Political Risk and Trade Credit Insurance: A U.K. Legal Perspective

Tony George and Carol Searle

Introduction

"Private" political risk insurance (PRI)—as opposed to state-sponsored or multilateral PRI, as placed in the London insurance market—in its wider definition comprises (a) cover for losses caused to investments and projects by government confiscation, expropriation, and nationalization (CEND, or PRI strictly speaking); and (b) insurance against contract frustration or repudiation (CF) by government obligors. More recently, structured trade credit has been insured against both CEND and CF risks, and straightforward counterparty default (cover provided by trade credit insurance (TCI) has been embraced within the term.[1]

The PRI market has undergone several claims cycles over the years since it started: the Middle East petrodollar boom and the Iranian revolution in the 1970s, the 1980s debt crisis, and the collapse of the USSR and the Balkan crisis in the 1990s, among others. In 2001/02, Argentina came to the fore. Since 2007, "resource nationalism," particularly in South America, has been resurgent.

This chapter examines the current claims environment and prospects for recoveries. How has this market been affected by the 2008 financial crisis, and what claims issues have arisen as a result?

Over recent years, the biggest users of the PRI market in London have been the banks—particularly banks specializing in trade finance. Most such banks were not affected by the first phase of the credit crunch in August 2007. In September 2008, however, with the collapse of Lehman Brothers, the crisis of confidence worldwide had a severe impact on the global economy, and by November 2008, global trade had dropped significantly. In the private PRI sector, the market faced what was described as a tsunami of claims. Estimates varied of the total number of claims notifications made, the top hitting US$4 billion. Ultimately, many of these notifications did not turn into claims. The latest estimates for market claims paid and incurred in 2008/09 are just under US$2.5 billion, spread around the banking sector, agribusiness, commodities such as oil and metals, and shipbuilding. Most of the claims that have materialized have been straightforward TCI claims of the simple "obligor can't pay" variety, and they have been or will be paid in full and promptly.

In any case, this is a legally sophisticated market: both underwriters and brokers—sometimes the insured itself—know the business and are well versed in its intricacy, which means if lawyers are needed, then the issues with the claims and their commercial resolution have likely already been explored, and a dispute and confrontation is in the offing.

The sheer size, number, and complexity of some of the claims has meant that lawyers have been and will still become involved—usually initially brought in by the insurers, and thereafter, should problems be perceived, also by the insured. Not surprisingly, this is happening, and this type of dispute-resolution work has begun again. The claims cycle has come round, and after a relatively quiet period, the lawyers are acting on claims rather than drafting and commenting upon wordings.

What about the claims issues the London market now faces? Are they the same, or is anything new?

What Legal Issues Arise in PRI Claims?

The Commercial Court in London deals with insurance matters. It also deals with matters regarding contracts related to ships, carriage of cargo, the construction and performance of mercantile contracts, banking, international credit, contracts relating to aircraft, the purchase and sale of commodities, and the practice of arbitration and questions arising from arbitrations. However, approximately 70 percent of all cases in the Commercial Court are said to be settled before reaching a trial.[2] On a broad-brush basis, one can fairly say that this experience is representative of insurance cases as well, including those that are dealt with in arbitration. In other words, even for those cases that reach external lawyers, and in respect of which proceedings are commenced (be it in court or arbitration), prospects are good that the parties will reach a settlement at some stage in the proceedings before trial. This tendency is stimulated by the increased use of mediation as a way of promoting settlement.

Nonetheless, whether a disputed claim involves reaching a judgment in court or award in arbitration or is subject to dispute resolution proceedings and resolved by agreement, the same insurance law issues arise.

The Top Five Issues

Recently, an analysis was made of 10 years of reported law cases in England using Lloyd's Insurance Law Reports (the "red tops"). During the period 2000–09 there were 498 reported insurance and reinsurance cases. Of those,

381 involved direct insurance, and 117 involved reinsurance; 109 involved appeals from earlier decisions. If one approaches the statistics another way, of the 389 cases (498 − 109 = 389) excluding appeals, 143 involved procedural issues such as jurisdiction and conflict of laws, costs, insolvency, and arguments about arbitration and time limitation, leaving 246 substantive insurance and reinsurance cases.

The top five issues that went to trial and for which judgment was given—showing the number of cases in each category and the category's percentage of the total number of substantive cases—were as follows:

1. Misrepresentation and nondisclosure: 52 (21 percent)
2. Preconditions, conditions precedent, and warranties: 47 (19 percent)
3. Coverage (what is insured and what is excluded): 42 (17 percent)
4. Causation: 17 (7 percent)
5. Subrogation or contribution: 15 (6 percent)

For completeness, the following were next in line as top issues:

6. Fraud (at the claims stage): 14 (5.6 percent)
7. Negligence: 14 (5.7 percent)
8. Aggregation: 8 (3.3 percent)
9. Policy construction: 8 (3.3 percent)

PRI Claims

One should bear in mind that the principal forum for dispute resolution in political and trade credit risk insurance policies in the London market is arbitration—usually the London Court of International Arbitration. Nevertheless, as mentioned earlier, one can say the patterns in that forum are similar. The main issues that arise are misrepresentation and nondisclosure; the extent of the coverage; and preconditions, conditions precedent, and warranties. With trade credit risk insurance products and their broad terms, however, issues about the meaning of policy perils and exclusions are less likely to arise, though this category still features in PRI.

These have been the sort of problems dealt with arising in previous claims cycles in the sector during the commercial PRI market's 35-year history. Have current claims issues been of the same tenor?

Current Claims Issues

This time, the bulk of the claims arises out of trade credit insurance, and the majority of the claimant insureds are banks. Banks, it seems, have a different approach to doing business from either that of the insurer or indeed that of the traditional insured commodity trader. Banks have a "cash against documents" mentality. Bankers are used to financial instruments that respond on presentation of compliant documents or on first demand, such as letters of credit. They are not used to the conditionality, whether express or implied, of long insurance policy wordings.

Another feature of banking—in some countries more than others—is employment instability, particularly these days. Employees leave; they are posted to different departments and countries. Their companies are restructured. This situation can give rise to a lack of continuity with projects and deals that is not always encountered with other types of insureds.

Also having an effect is the width of a bank's interests. Responding to an insured default can have unwonted (and unwanted) results from a bank's perspective: reputational damage in an emerging, competitive market, or more concretely, triggering of cross-defaults on other instruments.

How do these features translate into claims issues? With trade credit insurance and its basic cover for counterparties that cannot or will not pay, issues with coverage have been rare. The same old issues, however, have continued to arise.

Allegations of Nondisclosure and Misrepresentation

Arguments about what was told and should have been told to the underwriter on placement of the risk will always occur, but an increased feature arises with policy renewals and amendments. Underlying contracts in a recession are often renegotiated and payments rescheduled: generally, these are significant contract amendments. Maybe because they are used to operational risks and the need to keep their insurers in the picture with regard to changes in circumstances, this issue has not been a huge problem with insured traders, contractors, and corporate parties generally. With an insured bank, however, perhaps because it has not seen the need or because the policy has been metaphorically placed in the bottom drawer by an account handler who may have moved on, a greater risk seems to exist that its insurers are not advised, or fully or accurately advised, of the amendment. If the insurers are not advised, this failure could be a breach of warranty. If they are not fully or accurately advised, this failure could be nondisclosure or misrepresentation to underwriters, thus undermining the validity of any policy endorsement or renewal.

Warranties

Instances of a casual attitude toward checking the viability of deals have also been noted—the subprime mortgage syndrome. "Due diligence" in the corporate sense is lacking. Even though such deals may pass the credit committee review, when they come to be insured they run the risk of being in breach of warranties of validity and enforceability, and sometimes even legality.

Preparation and Presentation of Claims

More practically, problems have arisen in the preparation and presentation of claims documentation to insurers. It may be a product of the age of electronic communication and the employment volatility and restructuring mentioned earlier, but banks, in particular, seem to lack an appreciation of what insurers require in support of a claim and what they may want to satisfy themselves of its legitimacy. Linked with the perennial uncertainty an insured has about the role of the adjusters, at best this problem delays settlement (in any case, a topical issue at the moment), and at worst it creates suspicion in the minds of the insurers, leading to their hiring lawyers. This situation could also come to involve more use of the provision of a "sworn proof of loss" and the insured's executives having to submit to "examination under oath," as required under some wordings.

The Waiting Period

In the same vein, insureds seem to lack understanding about the purpose of this fundamental CF and trade credit insurance policy provision. This waiting period provision may be due for rethinking—at least about its title. One senses that an insured bank is under the impression that literally all it has to do is to wait to get its claim paid, not that it is under a continuing duty to avoid or minimize the loss in the exercise of due diligence—a concept that means something else in the world of finance anyway. Perhaps the principle of the insured peril of protracted default used in some trade finance covers should gain greater currency. A fresh approach to this concept might help with another problem being seen, which is peculiar to this class of business and which does not feature in the top five, but which is addressed below.

Crystallization of Loss

Problems are arising regarding the effect on the policy of debt standstills and reschedulings—or the reverse, acceleration of debt and implementation of cross-default clauses. Various questions arise:

- Does the insured have a crystallized claim when by virtue of commercial reality (or host government coercion), it has to accept a moratorium on payment or debt rescheduling?
- Is the answer different if the moratorium or rescheduling occurs after the original default but during the policy waiting period?
- Does the insured have to seek an extension of the policy when the new payment dates fall outside the original policy period? If so, does it have to pay an additional premium for such an extension, and how is it to be calculated, having in mind the original risk has deteriorated? (And bear in mind also the new duty of disclosure that then arises.)

Then:

- Upon default under the insured instrument, can the insured exercise any contractual acceleration rights in respect of later installments falling due and claim them under the policy when they are then not met?

- Can the insured exercise cross-default clauses under other instruments uninsured or insured elsewhere, and then assert claims if the insured debt so generated is not paid?
- Broadly, how do these rights square with the insured's express duties to avoid and minimize loss?

Certain general principles have been clarified during past recessions and individual country defaults, but the answers are likely to vary from policy wording to wording.

Settlement Agreements

Finally, developments have been observed with settlement agreements. Perhaps because of perceived shortcomings in claims preparation; perhaps simply a sort of reverse Micawberism—that "something may turn up" to establish that the insurers are not in fact liable—or perhaps insurers do not trust their insured to cooperate in the pursuit of subrogated recoveries as much as they should, but a change in practice on executing settlement and subrogation agreements has been seen on occasion. Insurers have insisted on detailed settlement terms upon payment of the claim. Sometimes even with straightforward claims being paid in full, the insured is asked to sign a four- or five-page document requiring it to agree to terms that go further than required by the policy wording.

The Effect of the Current Claims

Although not strictly a lawyer's concern, four often-related consequences of the crisis are seen in the private market:

- Reinsurance
- Capacity
- Products and wordings
- Recoveries.

Reinsurance and Capacity

Recently, a high-profile departure from the sector has occurred. But otherwise, as often happens after a period of intense claims activity, new entrants and new capacity have arrived—and this despite some contraction in reinsurance availability at one end of the spectrum (though not as much as was anticipated) and a loss of "liquid appetite" on the part of trade finance banks. On a per policy basis, however, one sees a re-emphasis on coinsurance, deductibles, and excesses.

Products and Wordings

A greater emphasis is now understood to be occurring on confining TCI to "trade proper"—the actual sale of physical goods and their financing. One must also place a question mark on whether this is the time for marketing new insurance products, when demand is reduced and many parts of the world are virtually off risk. Requests to consider the implications of tighter (if you are an insurer) or less favorable (if you are an insured) wordings have already arisen. In any case, a tension must be maintained between providing Basel II–compliant policies and writing policies with more insurer-oriented wordings.

Basel II itself raises interesting issues. So far, the policies designed to provide financial institutions with credit risk mitigation and capital relief have generally performed well, but what might happen if some high-profile disputes result in rejection of liability? The ultimate arbiters of capital allowances, the regulators, may be more skeptical about TCI as a credit risk mitigant and undermine the product's marketability. All this is of course based on the assumption that, at least in the medium term, Basel II survives while the financial community grapples with the prospect of a Basel III convention.

In considering tougher wordings, one must also not lose sight of the imminent recommendations for commercial insurance of the English and Scottish Law Commissions. Whether their recommendations will be implemented in the near future is a moot point, but they are likely to recommend changes to English insurance law that are on balance likely to be pro-insured—if only to stave off more radical legislation from the European Union.

Recoveries

Finally, the issue of recoveries surfaces as the claims tidal wave recedes. Traditionally, the profitability of the London market in this sector has been supported by the high rate of return on recoveries—in a strict PRI context, the attachment of the counterparty's foreign assets; the bilateral treaty award; and the use of specialists in unorthodox recovery processes. One hears of recovery rates of the order of one-third.

With TCI subrogation, however, one is not convinced such optimism should prevail. Most of the claims are of the "can't pay," not the "won't pay," variety. Insurers may now find themselves having to rank as the equivalent of a creditor in a perhaps debtor-skewed jurisdiction and involved in a winding-up process competing against other creditors who often have greater priority.

Concluding Comments

From the perspective of legal advisers in the London PRI market, one has reason to be confident that the private sector market in London has survived this claims cycle, and it has done so with an enhanced reputation given its positive response to claims to date. In the medium term, it can take advantage of the loss of credibility of the collateralized debt obligation and, more particularly, the credit default swap as a means to lay off risk.

Nonetheless, this sector of the market has suffered enormous losses, and there are lessons to be learned. Within the confines of a possible general U.K.

insurance law reform or EU legislation, one can expect a review (already under way in Lloyd's) and possible tightening up of policies and their terms, as well as a more rigorous approach to the identity and nature of insureds and their business.

Notes

1. Cover may also be provided for losses caused by political violence, including terrorism.

2. This figure is for the year to June 2007, referred to in the "Report and Recommendations if the Commercial Court Long Trials Working Party" (Judiciary of England and Wales London, December 2007), with a note that it "has not varied much over recent years" (p. 14).

CHAPTER 5

Investment Treaties and International Centre for Settlement Investment Disputes: What Investment Insurers Need to Know

Sabine Konrad

Investments are subject to various risks. Political changes may lead to modifications of tax laws or energy policies and to abandonment of infrastructural or regional development projects. Accordingly, the political backdrop and conditions under which an investment decision was made can change dramatically during the lifetime of the investment. In the worst-case scenario such changes can lead to a failure of the entire investment (Konrad 2008, 322).

Investments in foreign countries are subject to greater risks than are trade relationships or even investments in the investor's home jurisdiction. There are three reasons for this: (a) *ratione materiae*, which distinguishes trade from investment; (b) *ratione personae*, which distinguishes national investors from foreigners; and (c) the lack of democratic accountability.

The first risk factor is that the foreign investor typically brings its investment (and perhaps even itself) under the sovereign power of a foreign State. In a trade situation, however, that exposure is limited to the individual cross-border shipments.

The second risk factor stems from the fact that the burden of a certain government action may fall on the investor, whereas benefits accruing to nationals of the host State from the same, or another, compensatory government action may not benefit the investor. That is the case, for example, if the State increases taxes on corporate proceeds to finance national health care or a pension system (Konrad 2008, 322).

The last risk factor is the lack of democratic accountability. As the European Court of Human Rights observed, the host State government has been elected without the investor's participation.[1] This risk factor has two aspects: one constitutional and one political. As a matter of constitutional theory, the national—as member of the electorate—has elected the government and its political programme.[2] Second, as a matter of politics, the national can hold the government accountable at the next ballot. Put bluntly, if politicians' policies put an excessive burden on their citizens, politicians run the risk losing the next election. Taking from foreigners—expropriation without representation—will, most likely, not have the same effect on election results.

Deficits in democratic accountability and a lack of compensatory benefits for foreign investors make investors vulnerable. Several legal, political, and economical mechanisms have been created to provide certain protections against these risks, however. Perhaps most important ones are bilateral investment treaties (BITs) and multilateral investment treaties (MITs) between home and host States (Konrad 2008, 322). They work hand in hand with another important tool of investment protection—investment insurance provided by international organisations (such as Multilateral Investment Guaranty Agency),[3] State agencies (such as PricewaterhouseCoopers and Euler Hermes or the Export Credits Guarantee Department, United Kingdom),[4] or private insurers.[5]

Why Should an Investment Insurer Care?

The practical relevance of investment protection law for the safeguarding of investment projects is much higher than commonly perceived. The definition of "investment" in most modern investment protection treaties covers the majority of investment projects. In addition, several governments provide their foreign investors with insurance against political risks. Some of these countries, such as Germany, make government-sponsored political risk insurance contingent on the investment being covered by an investment treaty (Konrad 2008, 322–23).[6]

Moreover, investment protection significantly influences the risk analysis necessary to obtain financing for the project. It especially influences the applicable interest rate.

The issue of investment protection is relevant not only after difficulties arise, but also during project development. Bad decisions in the planning phase of the project often cannot be corrected after a conflict has arisen. Thus, considering issues of investment protection at an early stage of the project helps avoid conflicts or at least control the fallout.

Protection Available to the Insurer's Clients

The protection available to clients of investment insurers ultimately benefits the insurer. The existence of a BIT or an MIT contributes substantially to the investment climate in a foreign country, because it obliges the host State to provide a high standard of treatment vis-à-vis the foreign investor which strengthens the rule of law in the host State and thereby improves the overall conditions. Moreover, the most important of the substantive rights included in such treaties—the right to investor-State arbitration—gives the protections teeth. It allows the investor (and in turn the insurer) to recoup damages for a violation of one of the other substantive protections.

Investment treaties also have a political dimension; they lead to a depoliticization of disputes. The investor itself can enforce the rights provided under the treaty rather than having to rely on its home State to take action against the host State (which may not be politically opportune given the overall relationship between the two States).

In short, investment treaties mitigate political risk.

How Can the Insurer Recover What It Has Paid Out?

When an investment guarantee has to be paid out by the insurer, most investment treaties provide mechanisms for insurers to recover monies expended. There are two mechanisms through which recovery can be achieved: subrogation clauses and so-called "no-objection" clauses. Subrogation clauses empower the insurer (or the home State) to enforce claims against the host State in its own right. Depending on the scope of the subrogation clause in question, both public and private insurers may be covered. No-objection clauses allow the investor to pursue its rights under the treaty despite having received compensation from the insurer.

Although one can expect at least one subrogation or no-objection clause in a treaty, many treaties contain both types and allow the investor and the insurer to choose.

No-objection Clauses

No-objection clauses provide that if an investor has been indemnified under an insurance scheme, the investor may continue to exercise its rights under the BIT and claim damages irrespective of any payments it may have received from the insurer. The insurer may choose to contribute to the legal costs of pursuing the claims. Under the insurance contract, the insurer will then be reimbursed by the insured.

State practice with regard to no-objection clauses is largely similar,[7] with the exception of the Netherlands. The Dutch Model BIT does not contain a no-objection clause.[8]

Subrogation Clauses

Subrogation clauses allow an investment insurer that has issued investment insurance to commence arbitral proceedings in its own right. The host country must recognize the subrogation. However, State practice in observing the treaties differs as to which insurers can benefit from a subrogation. Moreover, sometimes there may be a question of nationality. Must the insurer have the same nationality as the insured to benefit from a subrogation? Is an insurance contract itself an investment?

State practice differs on the availability of subrogation. In some countries, the beneficiary of the subrogation is not the State insurer; rather, it is the home State itself. This is the case for German and French BITs.[9] Moreover, French BITs even require the host State's consent if an investor wants to buy insurance coverage.[10] Therefore, under French and German BITs, there is no "insurer-State" arbitration. Instead, the combined effect of the subrogation and no-objection clauses for those treaties is a choice between investor-State arbitration (under the no-objection clause) and State-State arbitration (under the subrogation clause).

Canadian, Finish, and UK BITs, as well as the Energy Charter Treaty, provide that the insurance agency of the home State (or the home State itself) is subrogated and then entitled to exercise and enforce the rights of the investor.[11]

Some BITs do not refer to insurance being provided by a "contracting party" (or its agency); instead, they refer to an insurer who provides insurance under a "system established by law."[12] One can argue that this provision also covers subrogation of rights to private insurers. In this situation, whether the insurer commencing arbitration and the insurer must be the same nationality as the investor is a question that has not yet arisen.

In U.S. BIT practice, however, subrogation is not provided for in the investment treaty itself but is covered in a separate Overseas Private Investment Corporation (OPIC) agreement. This practice may be one reason the United States has significantly fewer investment treaties than other capital exporting States. The United States has concluded only 53 investment treaties and free trade agreements, compared to more than 150 OPIC agreements.

How Does It Work?

Investment treaties do not offer protection against all kinds of risk, especially economic risks. Instead, they offer protection against political risks that are per se outside of the investor's scope of influence and control, because these risks emanate from the political sphere of the host State.

An investment decision depends on the confidence of the investor that the investment can and will create an expected return. To achieve this return, the investor calculates economic risks and structures the investment accordingly. Like every economic actor that deals at arms length in a free market environment and among other economic actors, the investor bears the economic risks of its investment. Investment treaties are not designed to guarantee the investor a specific return.

However, the circumstances under which the investor operates can be unilaterally changed by the host State in pursuit of the State's political goals. In some parts of the world, the political landscape is subject to high fluctuation because of frequent government changes. Permits and authorizations that formed the basis of the investment decision might be revoked, or a contract between the host State and the investor might not be honoured. As a result, the sovereign power of the host State places the investor in a position that does not guarantee that the investor can continue to operate at arms length in the market.

Investment treaties establish an international standard of good governance and protect the rule of law. They are typically concluded for a long period of time. Some have been in force for decades and have proven to be flexible enough to be "living instruments" capable of dealing with "present-day conditions"—a dictum coined by the European Court of Human Rights.[13]

Like human rights, investment treaties protect and contribute to the international rule of law, and these substantive protections would be meaningless without an effective enforcement mechanism. Therefore, modern investment treaties contain a dispute settlement clause, which allows the investor to initiate arbitration against the host State in an international forum. Unlike the national courts of the host State, international arbitration is a venue free from actual or perceived governmental influence. Moreover, the awards can be more easily enforced in other countries.

Important Protections in Investment Treaties: An Overview

Many of the rights contained in modern investment treaties were originally derived from customary international laws concerning the treatment of aliens in a foreign country. However, modern investment treaties have evolved and have, in turn, informed customary international law.

The greatest achievement of investment treaties is providing for the investor's right to access to international arbitration. Before that, an investor, as a private entity, could not initiate arbitration against a sovereign State without a special, individual agreement between the State and the private party. Investor-State arbitration continues to be consent based: consent of both parties is a necessary prerequisite. However, today, the most important source for consent of the host State is an investment treaty with the home State of the investor. The consent is given as a standing offer of both States vis-à-vis investors of the other State (Gaillard 2003, 2007).[14] To perfect the agreement to arbitrate, the investor needs to accept this offer. A host State also can make a standing offer to arbitrate in a national law.[15] In addition, consent may, of course, also be contained in a contract between the investor and the host State.[16] Regarding standing offers investment treaties have advantages over national laws: national laws can be changed unilaterally and sometimes even without warning.

Another important guarantee is the fair and equitable treatment standard (FET). Fair and equitable is an important element of the rule of law. For example, it covers the right to legal protection and the right to a fair trial[17] as well as the obligation of the State to act transparently[18] and predictably.[19] Often, a violation of legitimate expectations of the investor constitutes unfair and inequitable treatment and, thus, a violation of the FET standard.[20] FET is closely connected to the standard of full protection and security (OECD 2004, 26).

National treatment and most favoured nation treatment (MFN) are important standards to protect the foreign investor from discrimination. They are often combined with a provision prohibiting discriminatory or arbitrary conduct. A right to national treatment means that the host State may not subject the investor to treatment less favourable than it accords to its own investors. MFN mandates that the host State cannot subject the investor to treatment less favourable than it accords to investors of any third State.[21]

There are, however, limits on MFN. For example, according to so-called "REIO clauses,"[22] investors from a nonmember State of a REIO have no right to invoke the additional benefits enjoyed by nationals of the organization's member States under the law of such organization.[23] Moreover, an MFN clause may also stipulate that most favoured nation treatment is unavailable when it conflicts with a double taxation agreement.[24]

One of the oldest standards in customary international law is the protection against expropriation without compensation (Konrad 2008, 333). The State is free to expropriate the investor if certain conditions are met. The most important condition is that the State pays "prompt, adequate and effective compensation" (Konrad 2008, 334–35). The value of the investment for which compensation must be paid is usually assessed by determining the value of the investment directly before the decision to expropriate has become public. This practice generally does not present a problem when there has been a direct expropriation. However, when an investor has been the victim of indirect or creeping expropriation resulting from several measures of the host State which collectively or individually constitute an expropriation, it is more difficult to determine the value of the investment (Konrad 2008, 335). These issues require a case-by-case assessment of the facts.

Another important treaty provision is the so-called "umbrella clause" that appears in most investment treaties.[25] According to this kind of provision, the host State of an investment "shall observe any other obligation it has assumed with regard to investments in its territory by investors of the other Contracting State."[26] While this wording leaves no doubt that it is, in fact, an umbrella clause, other formulations which are far less clear can be found in treaty practice.[27]

Umbrella clauses protect contracts between the investor and the host State. They apply to contractual or other reciprocal commitments by the host State but also to unilateral undertakings. They are modelled on the generally recognized principle of international law of *pacta sunt servanda*, which applies between States. Umbrella clauses transpose this principle to the investor-State level.

The origins of the umbrella clause can be traced to the Abs/Shawcross Draft Convention on Foreign Investment in the 1950s. Its aim was to respond to the needs of an increasingly globalized world economy and to close important gaps in the protection of foreign investments. Now, almost all European investment treaties and the Energy Charter Treaty contain such clauses. By virtue of the umbrella clause, a violation of the contract also constitutes a separate violation of the treaty. Accordingly, the umbrella clause makes the treaty dispute settlement mechanism available to enforce obligations of the host State with respect to investments.[28]

Umbrella clauses are of particular importance for all projects in which public authorities of the host State are involved, especially infrastructure projects. The traditional protections of fair and equitable treatment and the prohibition of expropriation without compensation may be less efficient to protect the investor against interference. Similarly, the investment contract with the State may not provide sufficient protection, especially if it is often governed by local law and provides for redress only to local courts under the control of the host State.

The understanding that the umbrella clause connects the realm of national law with the realm of international law and thus "internationalizes" contract violations has not been undisputed in arbitral practice, however.[29] Although certain difficulties persist, most arbitral tribunals agree that the umbrella clause must be given effect and that contract violations can be examined in investment treaty arbitration (see, for example, OECD 2006, 22).

Investment Treaty Arbitration under the Auspices of International Centre for Settlement of Investment Disputes

As explained earlier, investment treaties provide for substantive rights, one of which is the right to access investor-State arbitration. There are a number of fora available for this kind of arbitration: arbitration under the International Centre for Settlement of Investment Disputes (ICSID) Convention, other institutional arbitration, and ad hoc arbitration.

ICSID is a member of the World Bank Group and came into existence when the Convention on the Settlement of Investment Disputes between States and Nationals of Other States entered into force on March 18, 1966 (ICSID Convention).[30] Arbitrations conducted under the auspices of the ICSID Convention are supported by the ICSID Secretariat. Awards rendered according to the ICSID Convention enjoy various privileges at the enforcement stage (see below). This makes ICSID a very effective means of pursuing investor-State claims.

According to Article 25 of the ICSID Convention, the jurisdiction of the Centre extends to "any legal dispute between a contracting State (or any constituent subdivision or agency of a Contracting State designated to the Centre) and a national of another contracting State, which the parties consent in writing to submit to the Centre." While the notion of a "National of another Contracting State" is explicitly defined in Article 25(2) of the ICSID Convention, the term "investment" is not, which has led to much debate.

Because economic life develops at fast pace and continuously invents new forms of businesses and investments, the definition of investment in an investment treaty must be flexible. Otherwise, an investment treaty would be outdated before it can even be ratified. Most investment treaties therefore define the term "investment" in a very broad sense as "every kind of asset" followed by a nonexhaustive list. Some have argued that despite the Convention's silence, it requires additional elements to be present.[31] Without these elements, the investor may be able to initiate arbitration in another forum, but not under the ICSID Convention. Others have pointed out that such elements may be describing common characteristics of an investment while not constituting requirements or amounting to a definition.[32]

As explained earlier, consent is the cornerstone for access to arbitration (Gaillard 2007, 7). It can be given in a treaty, in national legislation, or in a contract.[33] This consent will constitute a binding offer for ICSID arbitration even if the State later denounces the ICSID Convention.

Arbitration under the ICSID Convention is special in that it provides for a self-contained system. This means that awards rendered under the ICSID Convention are not subject to remedies before national courts of the member States and cannot be set aside by them. Instead, there is a specific annulment mechanism under the ICSID Convention which permits the annulment of awards on very limited grounds. According to Article 52 of the ICSID Convention, these grounds are (a) the tribunal was not properly constituted, (b) the tribunal has manifestly exceeded its powers, (c) there was corruption on the part of a member of the tribunal, (d) there has been a serious departure from a fundamental rule of procedure, or (e) the award has failed to state the reasons on which it is based. Although the number of both ICSID awards and applications for annulment of ICSID awards has grown in recent years, only a very limited number of these awards has actually been annulled. As of April 2011, only 11 awards had been annulled in full or in part.[34]

The principle of exclusivity of ICSID arbitration also has implications for the enforcement of ICSID awards. According to Article 53 of the ICSID Convention (and pertinent provisions in an investment treaty), the parties must abide by an award. However, Article 54 of the ICSID Convention extends the binding effect beyond the parties to the arbitration. Not only the respondent State (and the investor) but also the other member States of the ICSID Convention must recognize an award as binding and enforce its pecuniary obligations as if it were a final judgment of its own national courts. This privilege of enforcement does not transpose into a privilege of execution, however. As for final judgments of national courts, their execution is governed by the pertinent laws of the State. This includes the laws relating to State immunity.

Nevertheless, the failure of a State to meet its obligation to comply with an award under the ICSID Convention would constitute a violation of Article 53 of the Convention and the investment treaty (Schreuer et al. 2009, 33–38). State immunity laws cannot shield it from that liability.

Other Fora for Investment Treaty Arbitration

Apart from ICSID, there are a number of other fora for institutional arbitration. These include arbitration pursuant to ICSID's Additional Facility Rules,[35] the Stockholm Chamber of Commerce (SCC) Arbitration Rules,[36] or the International Chamber of Commerce (ICC)[37] Arbitration Rules. Ad hoc arbitrations are often conducted according to the UNCITRAL (United Nations Commission on International Trade Law) Arbitration Rules.[38]

In all cases of non-ICSID arbitration, including the Additional Facility Rules, the award does not enjoy the privilege of enforcement conferred by the ICSID Convention. Arbitration awards outside ICSID are normally enforced under the 1958 Convention on the Recognition and Enforcement of Foreign Arbitral Awards (also referred to as the "New York Convention").

Does It Work?

Winston Churchill's remark[39] about democracy could easily be adapted to investment treaty arbitration: it is not "perfect or all-wise." Some may, perhaps, even say that it "is the worst form of international dispute resolution." But it is important to add Churchill's caveat: "except for all those other forms that have been tried from time to time."

Some cases are settled quickly, while others can take many years to resolve. For example, *Ed. Zueblin AG v. Saudi Arabia* was settled shortly after it was registered,[40] whereas *Vivendi v. Argentina* was registered in 1997 and was concluded only in 2010 after two annulment proceedings.[41]

The length of time between registration of a case and rendering of an award also varies dramatically. For example, in *ADC v. Hungary*, a final award was rendered after only three years.[42] The case of *Victor Pey Casado v. Chile* was registered in 1998, and, as of June 2011, annulment proceedings are still pending.[43]

Like any type of dispute resolution, investment treaty arbitration can yield results fast and relatively cost-efficient; or it can end up in a long, expensive, protracted dispute. However, what matters is that, from a practical perspective, investment treaty arbitration in principle serves its function and compares favourably to other means of dispute resolution.

Moreover, there is no real alternative to investment treaty arbitration. The exercise of diplomatic protection by the home State is dependent on political circumstances and the general relationship between the two States. Because of the diplomatic implications of an intervention, the home State will often choose not to intervene on behalf of the investor. Whether or not the investor has a right to diplomatic protection under the law of the home State is a matter of national law. In addition, the investor may be required to exhaust domestic remedies to achieve an intervention, and even if the investor ultimately is successful, the home State has discretion how it exercises diplomatic protection and whether it will take effective steps.

Although Article 27 of the ICSID Convention excludes diplomatic protection once a dispute is submitted to ICSID arbitration, it does not prohibit diplomatic assistance in solving a dispute amicably. Similarly, conciliation and mediation sometimes lead to the settlement of disputes. All of these options can play an important role in avoiding arbitration proceedings and can often be very successful. One of the most important reasons for this success is that the investor can still go to international arbitration if an amicable solution is not possible. Conciliation or mediation would be far less successful without the ultimate option of treaty arbitration. Thus, they are complementary to treaty arbitration, but not substitutes for it.

Human rights proceedings (for example, under the European Convention on Human Rights) also are an option for the investor to receive a final and binding judgment. However, these proceedings require the exhaustion of local remedies.[44] Outside Europe, human rights proceedings also are not available to companies.[45] As mentioned earlier, investment treaties were developed specifically to avoid the requirement to exhaust local remedies. Moreover, protection under BITs is available to all individuals and entities with the requisite nationality, including companies.

Investment treaty arbitration gives the investor a right to arbitration against the host State without regard to politics or the investor's relationship with its home government. Investment treaties are in line with the increased protection of private entities against States in international law. As such, they provide a tool for protecting and empowering individuals and other non-State players and constitute an important complement of international human rights law.

Conclusion: What Is Important in Particular for an Investment Insurer?

Investment insurers usually get involved very early in the life cycle of an investment. Thus, they are in an almost unparalleled position to make sure that the insured investment is structured in a way to be protected by an investment treaty. This guarantee will reduce the insurer's own exposure and—especially if only a part of the investment is insured—the risk for the investor. Indeed, investment protection planning is as important as tax planning. Legitimate corporate structuring of the investment can optimize protection (Konrad 2008, 363). Although an insurer may not be able to provide advice, it can highlight points for the investor that then need to be explored with the investor's counsel.

Moreover, investment protection planning does not stop once the investment is made. The protection must consider changes during the lifetime of the project, for example, changes in host State legislation, on the treaty level, and changes in the nationality of the investor. If the project is not protected or loses protection, an investor cannot expect to achieve full (or sometimes any) recovery (Konrad 2008, 366). Therefore, investment protection for the investor translates into an increased chance of the insurer to recover monies it paid under political risk insurance.

Careful drafting of a foreign direct investment contract with a State-owned entity is equally important. Receiving input from an experienced insurer that may have an understanding of contracts customarily used by a certain government may be helpful to reduce risks for the investor.

Investment treaties are an important and indispensable tool in international economic relations.

Notes

1. European Court of Human Rights, No. 9006/80, *Lithgow v. United Kingdom*, Judgment of July 8, 1986, 115. See Konrad (2007, 323–24).

2. This is irrespective of whether or not the individual national has voted with or against the majority. It is a consequence of the concept of representative democracy.

3. For more information, see http://www.miga.org.

4. For more information, see http://www.agaportal.de/en/dia/index.html, and http://www.ecgd.gov.uk.

5. A list of the most important political risk insurers is available at http://www.berneunion.org.uk/bu_profiles.htm.

6. For more information, see http://www.agaportal.de/en/dia/index.html.

7. See, for example, the German 2009 Model BIT, Article 10 ("(5) During arbitration proceedings or the enforcement of an award, the Contracting State involved in the dispute shall not raise the objection that the investor of the other Contracting State has received compensation under an insurance contract in respect of all or part of the damage."); the U.S. 2004 Model BIT, Article 28 ("7. A respondent may not assert as a defense, counterclaim, right of set-off, or for any other reason that the claimant has received or will receive indemnification or other compensation for all or part of the alleged damages pursuant to an insurance or guarantee contract."); the U.K. 2008 Draft Model BIT, Article 8 ("3. … The Contracting Party which is a party to the dispute shall not raise as an objection at any stage of the proceedings or enforcement of an award the fact that the national or company which is the other party to the dispute has received in pursuance of an insurance contract an indemnity in respect of some or all of his or its losses."); and the Canadian 2004 Model BIT, Article 46 ("3. In an arbitration under this Section, a disputing Party shall not assert, as a defense, counterclaim, right of setoff or otherwise, that the disputing investor has received or will receive, pursuant to an insurance or guarantee contract, indemnification or other compensation for all or part of its alleged damages.").

8. For more information, see appendix 15 of the Netherlands 2004 Model BIT in McIlwrath and Savage (2010).

9. See, for example, the Agreement between the Federal Republic of Germany and the Islamic Republic of Pakistan on the Encouragement and Reciprocal Protection of Investments of December 1, 2009 (Germany-Pakistan BIT), Article 6 ("If either Contracting State makes a payment to any of its investors under its scheme of guarantees it has assumed in respect of an investment in the territory of the other Contracting State, the latter Contracting State shall, without prejudice to the rights of the former Contracting State under Article 9, recognize the assignment, whether under a law or pursuant to a legal transaction, of any right or claim of such investor to the former Contracting State."); Accord entre le Gouvernement de la République Française et le Gouvernement du Royaume D'arabie Saoudite sur l'encouragement et la Protection réciproques des Investissements de juin 26, 2002 (France-Saudi Arabia BIT), Article 7 ("Si l'une des Parties contractantes, en vertu d'une garantie donnée pour un investissement réalisé sur le territoire ou dans la zone maritime de l'autre Partie contractante, effectue des versements à l'un de ses investisseurs, elle est, de ce fait, subrogée dans les droits et actions de ces investisseurs. Lesdits versements n'affectent pas les droits des investisseurs à recourir aux procédures décrites à l'Article 6.").

10. Accord entre le Gouvernement de la République Française et le Gouvernement de l'état du Qatar sur l'Encouragement et la Protection réciproques des Investissements du 8 juillet 1996 (France-Qatar BIT), Article 7: "Dans la mesure où la réglementation de l'une des Parties contractantes prévoit une garantie pour les investissements effectués à l'étranger, celle-ci peut être accordée, dans le cadre d'un examen cas par cas, à des investissements effectués par des investisseurs de cette Partie sur le territoire ou dans la zone maritime de l'autre Partie. Les investissements des investisseurs de l'une des Parties contractantes sur le territoire ou dans la zone maritime de l'autre Partie ne pourront obtenir la garantie visée à l'alinéa ci-dessus que s'ils ont, au préalable, obtenu l'agrément de cette dernière Partie.").

11. See, for example, the Canadian 2004 Model BIT, Article 15 ("1. If a Party or any agency thereof makes a payment to any of its investors under a guarantee or a contract of insurance it has entered into in respect of an investment, the other Party shall recognize the validity of the subrogation in favor of such Party or agency thereof to any right or title held by the investor. 2. A Party or any agency thereof which is subrogated to the rights of an investor in accordance with paragraph 1 of this Article, shall be entitled in all circumstances to the same rights as those of the investor in respect of the investment. Such rights may be exercised by the Party or any agency thereof, or by the investor if the Party or any agency thereof so authorizes.").

12. See, for example, the Agreement on Encouragement and Reciprocal Protection of Investments between the Kingdom of the Netherlands and Jamaica) of April 18, 1991 (Netherlands-Jamaica BIT), Article 8 ("If the investment of a national of the other Contracting Party are insured against noncommercial risks under a system established by law, and the insurer or the re-insurer makes a payment or agrees to make a payment pursuant to the terms of such insurance, any subrogation of the insurer or the re-insurer into the rights of the said national shall be recognized by the other Contracting Party.").

13. See European Court of Human Rights, No. 5856/72, *Tyrer v. United Kingdom*, Judgment of April 25, 1978, 31.

14. Such consent may traditionally be given in an arbitration clause contained in a contract or through a compromise once the dispute has arisen. It may also be given separately by the host State and the investor, the latter accepting, at the time the dispute has arisen, the prior and general consent to arbitration given by the former in a provision of its domestic legislation or in an investment protection treaty.", Gaillard (2007, 7).

15. See, for example, *Tradex Hellas S.A. v. Republic of Albania*, ICSID Case No. ARB/94/2, Decision on Jurisdiction of December 24, 1996, *reprinted in* ICSID Review—Foreign Investment Law Journal (1999), Vol. 14, Issue 1, 186–87; *Petrobart Limited v. The Kyrgyz Republic*, SCC, Award of March 29, 2005, 73–74.

16. See, for example, *CDC Group PLC v. Republic of Seychelles*, ICSID Case No. ARB/02/14, Award of December 17, 2003, 3–4.

17. *Bayindir Insaat Turizm Ticaret Ve Sanayi A.S. v. Islamic Republic of Pakistan*, ICSID Case No. ARB/03/29, Award of August 27, 2009, 178; *Suez et al. v. Argentine Republic*, ICSID Case No. ARB/03/17, Award of July 30, 2010, 167.

18. *Maffezini v. Kingdom of Spain*, ICSID Case No. ARB/97/7, Award of November 13, 2000, 83.

19. *Metalclad Corporation v. Mexico,* ICSID Case No. ARB(AF)/97/1 (NAFTA), Award of August 30, 2000, 99.

20. *Tecnicas Medioambientales TECMED S.A. v. United Mexican States,* ICSID Case No. ARB(AF)/00/02, Award of May 29, 2003, 154; *Azurix Corp. v. The Argentine Republic,* ICSID Case No. ARB/01/12, Award of July 14, 2006, 372; *International Thunderbird Gaming Corporation v. The United Mexican States,* UNCITRAL (NAFTA), Award of January 26, 2006, 147.

21. For the application of MFN treatment to the right of access to international arbitration, see Konrad (2008, 338–39).

22. For Regional Economic Integration Organization, one of the most important REIOs is the European Union.

23. See, for example, the Agreement between the Republic of Turkey and the Kingdom of Denmark Concerning the Reciprocal Promotion and Protection of Investments of February 7, 1990 (Turkey-Denmark BIT), Article 3.3 ("The provisions of this Article shall have no effect in relation to international agreements entered into by either of the Contracting Parties: [a] relating to any existing or future customs union, regional economic organizations or similar international agreements, [b] relating wholly, or mainly to taxation.").

24. For example, Article 3 of the Agreement between Malaysia and Chile for the Promotion and Protection of Investments of 11 November 1992 (Chile-Malaysia BIT) provides: "The provision in this Treaty relating to treatment no less favorable than that accorded to investments of third States shall not be interpreted to oblige a Contracting Party to extend to investors of the other Contracting Party the benefits of any treatment, preference or privilege by virtue of … any international convention or agreement related totally or principally to taxation, or any national legislation related totally or partially to taxation."

25. See, for example, *Consorzio Groupement L.E.S.I.—DIPENTA v. People's Democratic Republic of Algeria,* ICSID Case No. ARB/03/8, Award of January 10, 2005, 25; see also Gaillard (2003, 853, 859 and note 43; 2005, 325–26, 336; 2010, 205–18, 274–84 and 423, 425–26).

26. See, for example, the Agreement between the Federal Republic of Germany and the Republic of India for the Promotion and Protection of Investments of July 10, 1995 (Germany-India BIT), Article 13(2); see also the German 2009 Model BIT, Article 7(2) (the host State "shall fulfill any other obligations it may have entered into with regard to investments in its territory by investors of the other Contracting State.").

27. See, for example, French Model 2006 BIT, Article 9 ("Investments having formed the subject of a special commitment of one Contracting Party, with respect to the nationals or companies of the other Contracting Party, shall be governed, without prejudice to the provisions of this Agreement, by the terms of the said commitment if the latter includes provisions more favorable than those of this Agreement. The provisions of article 8 of the present Agreement shall apply even in the case of a special commitment to the effect of waiving international arbitration or designating an arbitration body other than that mentioned in article 8 of the present Agreement."). The French version States in relevant part as follows: "Les investissements ayant fait l'objet d'un engagement particulier de l'une des Parties contractantes à l'égard des investisseurs de l'autre Partie contractante sont régis, sans préjudice des dispositions du présent accord, par les termes de cer engagement dans la mesure

où celui-ci comporte des dispositions plus favorables que celles qui sont prévues par le présent accord. Les dispositions de l'article 8 du présent Accord s'appliquent même en cas d'engagement spécifique prévoyant la renunciation a l'arbitrage international ou désignant une instance arbitrale différente de celle mentionnée à l'article 8 du présent Accord.").

28. In addition, umbrella clauses also serve an important function for the home State in State-State disputes.

29. See, for example, Konrad (2008, 341) for a discussion of the different interpretations.

30. Arbitration under ICSID requires that both the host State and the home State of the investor are members of the ICSID Convention. As of May 5, 2011, 147 States had deposited their instrument of ratification. See http://icsid.worldbank.org.

31. Among those who favor a catalogue of criteria, there is no agreement of the number of such constitutive elements. Some have identified three: *Consorzio Groupement L.E.S.I.-DIPENTA v. People's Democratic Republic of Algeria*, ICSID Case No. ARB/03/8, Award of January 10, 2005, 13–15; *Victor Pey Casado and President Allende Foundation v. Republic of Chile*, ICSID Case No. ARB/98/2, Award of May 8, 2008, 232. Others require four or even more, including a contribution to the host State's development: *Salini Costruttori S.p.A. v. Morocco*, ICSID Case No. ARB/00/4, Decision on Jurisdiction of July 23, 2001, 52; *Joy Mining Machinery Limited v. Arab Republic of Egypt*, ICSID Case No. ARB/03/11, Award on Jurisdiction of August 6, 2004, 53; *Jan de Nul N.V. and Dredging International N.V. v. Arab Republic of Egypt*, ICSID Case No. ARB/04/13, Decision on Jurisdiction of June 16, 2006, 91; *Patrick Mitchell v. The Democratic Republic of Congo*, ICSID Case No. ARB/99/7, Decision on the Stay of Enforcement of the Award of February 9, 2004, 29, 33.

32. See, for example, *Malaysian Historical Salvors, SDN, BHD v. Malaysia*, ICSID Case No. ARB/05/10, Decision on the Application for Annulment of April 16, 2009, 78; *Inmaris Perestroika Sailing Maritime Services GMBH and Others v. Ukraine*, ICSID Case No. ARB/08/8, Decision on Jurisdiction of March 8, 2010, 129; *Alpha Projektholding GmbH v. Ukraine*, ICSID Case No. ARB/07/16, Award of November 8, 2010, 311; *Biwater Gauff (Tanzania) Limited v. United Republic of Tanzania*, ICSID Case No. ARB/05/22, Award of July 24, 2008, 310, 312–18; see also Schreuer et al. (2009); for a comprehensive discussion, see Gaillard (2009).

33. Ratification of the ICSID Convention by the host and home States is insufficient to confer jurisdiction on a dispute (Schreuer et al. 2009, 379–81).

34. As of April 5, 2011, there have been 11 full or partial annulments compared to 302 registered cases, 130 awards, and 43 registered annulment proceedings (Kinnear 2011).

35. For more information, see http://icsid.worldbank.org/ICSID/ICSID/AdditionalFacilityRules.jsp.

36. For more information, see http://www.sccinstitute.com/skiljedomsregler-4.aspx.

37. For more information, see http://www.iccwbo.org/court/arbitration/id4199/index.html.

38. For the 1976 rules, see http://www.uncitral.org/pdf/english/texts/arbitration/arb-rules/arb-rules.pdf, and for the 2010 rules, see http://www.uncitral.org/pdf/english/texts/arbitration/arb-rules-revised/arb-rules-revised-2010-e.pdf. The 1976 rules will apply to most investment arbitrations.

39. In an address to the House of Commons, Churchill (1947) stated: "Many forms of Government have been tried, and will be tried in this world of sin and woe. No one pretends that democracy is perfect or all-wise. Indeed, it has been said that democracy is the worst form of government except all those other forms that have been tried from time to time."

40. Ed. *Züblin AG v. Kingdom of Saudi Arabia*, ICSID Case No. ARB/03/01, http://icsid. worldbank.org.

41. *Compania de Aguas del Aconquija S.A. and Vivendi Universal S.A. v. Argentine Republic*, ICSID Case No ARB/97/3, http://icsid.worldbank.org.

42. *ADC Affiliate Limited and ADC & ADMC Management Limited v. Republic of Hungary*, ICSID Case No. ARB/03/16, Award of the Tribunal, 2 October 2006, http://icsid.worldbank.org.

43. *Victor Pey Casado and President Allende Foundation v. Republic of Chile*, ICSID Case No. ARB/98/2, pending as of June 2011, http://icsid.worldbank.org.

44. Article 35(1) of the European Convention on the Protection of Human Rights and Fundamental Freedoms provides as follows: "The Court may only deal with [a] matter after all domestic remedies have been exhausted, according to the generally recognised rules of international law." See also Article 46(1)(a) of the American Convention on Human Rights of November 22, 1969, and Article 41(1)(c) of the International Covenant on Civil and Political Rights of December 16, 1966.

45. The entitlement of juridical persons to the protection of the European Convention on the Protection of Human Rights and Fundamental Freedoms has always been recognized, even if the only substantive protection which mentions "legal persons" explicitly is Article 1 of Protocol No. 1. Interestingly, the American Convention on Human Rights has been interpreted restrictively. Article 1, § 2, which defines "person" as "every human being," is read as limiting the scope of application also of those provisions of the convention which—like its Article 21—do not refer to "persons." For ways to mitigate the consequences, [see] Inter-American Court of Human Rights, *Cantos v. Argentina*, Judgment of September 7, 2001, 2001 Inter-Am. Ct. H.R. (ser. C) No. 85, 22–29; Inter-American Court of Human Rights, *Perozo v. Venezuela*, Judgment of January 28, 2009, 2009 Inter-Am. Ct. H.R. (ser. C), No. 195, 74 and 399. An even more restrictive approach has been adopted for the International Covenant on Civil and Political Rights (see Human Rights Committee, General Comment No. 31, The Nature of the General Legal Obligation Imposed on States Parties to the Covenant, 9, U.N. Doc. CCPR/C/21/Rev.1/Add.13).

CHAPTER 6

Sovereign Risk and Political Risk: New Challenges

Anne Marie Thurber and Samit Shah

This chapter describes what is meant by nonhonoring insurance coverage, why it is useful for insureds, how the market has changed over the years, what issues are important to underwriters and buyers of the coverage, and what recent developments have occurred in the aftermath of the global economic crisis. It then comments on several key considerations.

What Is Nonhonoring Coverage?

Essentially, nonhonoring coverage protects an insured against the failure of a government entity to honor its payment obligations. These obligations can arise as a result of commercial contracts or financing arrangements from lenders or capital market investors. In addition, a government entity can be the sovereign itself, a subsovereign (province or municipality), or a state-owned enterprise (SOE). The payment obligation can arise directly where the borrower is the sovereign federal government (usually through the ministry of finance), from a guaranty by the sovereign on behalf of another borrower, or from the obligation of a subsovereign (SS) or SOE.

When referring to nonhonoring coverage, the most straightforward structure is that in which a bank lends money to a sovereign borrower to fund the purchase of goods or services. Although the transaction is a key component, the obligation to repay the bank exists regardless of the results of the underlying contract. In this manner, the loan is "delinked" from the performance of the contractor or supplier. Thus, the obligation to repay is constant, but the resulting performance risk shifts to the sovereign because the loan proceeds were used to pay the contractor or supplier directly. If a problem arises with the underlying contract, because the contractor or supplier has already received the funds, the government must rely on other mechanisms to resolve the problem, such as calling on performance guaranties.

The performance risk can be shifted back to the contractor or supplier if a contractor or supplier is financing a commercial contract to provide goods or services to a government buyer. Depending upon how the agreements are structured, the contractor or supplier may take not only the payment risk for services delivered but also the contract risk in the event the contract is unilaterally terminated where the buyer had no right to do so, as well as for the usual political risks (embargo, license cancellation, political violence, and so on). Because of the specialized risks associated with the performance of the contract, the coverage is structured as contract frustration (CF). Although such coverage has specific underwriting considerations, the payment aspect is similar in approach to the more general nonhonoring approach.

Finally, government payment risk can arise under a commercial contract in which a government buyer agrees to buy or deliver goods or services on an ongoing basis, such as an agreement to purchase power. The coverage for this risk is generally structured as arbitration award default coverage. Although much of the analysis regarding the ability to pay is similar to that of nonhonoring, arbitration award default coverage involves many more considerations, such as the dispute resolution mechanism and the choice of law, that this chapter does not address.

Market for Nonhonoring Coverage

Historically, most sellers or lenders protected themselves against sovereign defaults by seeking support from their country's export credit agency through loan guarantees. As the demand for this protection has grown and because banks were more willing to take a portion of the risk on their own books, the private market developed an insurance product to respond to this growing need. The government and multilateral political risk insurers are now responding with their own insurance product offering as well. The insurance product is different from the loan guarantee in several important ways that are discussed below.

More recently, the global recession and subsequent downgrading of many countries has further boosted demand for nonhonoring insurance as customers look to mitigate country risk and to manage exposure. Whereas banks have pulled back from more risky classes of business, the secured nature of export finance and its historically low default rates have encouraged banks to focus more on sovereign borrowers. These trends in the banking market, along with a reduction in bank syndications, have resulted in increased demand for nonhonoring coverage from the insurance market. Also influencing demand was the reserving advantage that banks received with the addition of the more comprehensive payment coverage of the nonhonoring product. The implementation of Basel II also increased significantly the benefits to a bank purchasing nonhonoring coverage for those banks located in countries whose regulators recognized the protection.

In recent years, demand for nonhonoring coverage has demonstrated steady growth, although during the global financial crisis demand dipped as projects were placed on hold temporarily. Supply, however, has not been affected by the global financial crisis. In fact, according to the Multilateral Investment Guarantee Agency's *World Investment and Political Risk 2009* (MIGA 2010), the availability of political risk insurance (public and private) grew considerably from 2007 to 2009. This finding is confirmed by the July 2010 Gallagher London "Political Risks Insurance Report and Market Update," which focuses on the availability of coverage offered by the private sector. This report shows a marked increase in nonhonoring CF coverage from January to July 2008 with availability continuing to increase throughout the cycle. Of course, the amount available for any particular transaction depends on tenor because some private markets are restricted to tenors of three to five years.

Contrary to conventional wisdom, the private market did not reduce limits available for the nonhonoring product during the global financial crisis. In fact, while one underwriter exited the market, several new providers have entered with meaningful lines. Most private insurers view nonhonoring risk as relatively attractive. This view is supported by the impression that recovery prospects following claims payments on nonhonoring risks are quite good. Although not a comment on pricing specifically, the rate increases experienced over the past two years were caused by general volatility in the market, which led to higher spreads.

Interestingly, the global financial crisis has led to demand for nonhonoring coverage in countries where the market has not been active in many years, such as Greece, Iceland, and Spain, particularly with respect to SSs and SOEs. Although almost any risk can find a taker for the right price, the market for these risks is probably somewhat thin.

Nonhonoring Insurance Is Not a Guaranty

One must remember that the product available from public and private providers of political risk insurance is an insurance policy, not a financial guaranty or loan guaranty. The following are a few important differences: (a) the contingent nature of the obligation to pay, (b) the risk sharing, and (c) the insurer's expectation of the insured's behavior during the tenor of the policy.

On the first point, an insurance policy is a contingent obligation to pay. It will pay a proven loss if no exclusions apply and subject to certain other conditions. If there is a default of a covered scheduled payment, the default triggers a waiting period—generally 180 days. After the waiting period has expired, the insured then has the opportunity to file a claim. The underwriter engages in claim adjustment activities that include verification of a loss under the policy and verification that representations, warranties, and duties were correct and undertaken to the best of the insured's capabilities. In addition, the documentation must be legal and enforceable at the time of the claim.

On the second point, the insurance is a risk-sharing product. Indemnities range up to 95 percent for sovereign obligations and generally up to 90 percent for SSs, including SOEs. In addition to a portion of the risk being retained by the insured for its own account, the underwriter expects the insured not only to act in the best interests as if "uninsured" but also to act on behalf of the underwriter after consultation with the underwriter. Obviously this duality requires extensive communication between the insured and the underwriter, further emphasizing the risk-sharing aspect of the coverage.

This discussion leads to the third point—the insured's behavior. Particularly for private sector underwriters, in the event of a default and after a claim is paid, the expectation is that the insured will continue to act on behalf of the underwriter in attempting to recover amounts that have been paid to the insured. Different underwriters participate to varying degrees in formulating strategies to effect recoveries.

Underwriting Considerations

The type of transaction, the nature of the borrower, and the underlying project all influence the attractiveness of the risk to the underwriter.

The most straightforward of applications is that in which a bank lends to the sovereign government for a particular project. In this case, ideally the borrower is the ministry of finance, but in some cases the underwriter may be willing to accept another agency of the sovereign government (for example, the ministry of health). In all cases, the underwriter must assure itself that the entity binding the government actually has the legal ability to do so. Assuming that the repayment of the loan is dissociated from the performance of the underlying contract, the insurer wants to be comfortable with the use of the proceeds; that is, is the project an appropriate use of government funds? Some may view the financing of a hospital to be less risky than the financing of a resort or the presidential plane.

The underwriting in this simplified case would involve assessing the ability of the sovereign to pay the loan over time as well as its willingness to do so. Reports from rating agencies and the International Monetary Fund (IMF) may assist the underwriter in assessing ability to pay, but assessing willingness requires more of the "art" of the political risk insurance underwriter. The insured takes a predominant role in the underwriting assessment. Underwriting the insured seems to take on more importance to the private sector underwriter than the public sector underwriter. Perhaps this difference is caused by the assumption that in any difficult situation, the private underwriter relies to a greater extent on the insured to act on its behalf than the public sector underwriter. Also, the market experience has demonstrated that insureds who are practiced in emerging markets and have a strong prior relationship with the borrower can better work through the bumps that arise along the road.

From the public sector's point of view, an assessment of the project seems to be of more importance.

The more challenging underwriting involves SSs and SOEs. An SS is a regional, local, or municipal entity that lacks the full faith and credit of the sovereign. An SOE is an entity that is more than 50 percent owned by a government (or governmental organization) or controlled by the government, or in some cases, an entity whose existence is deemed to be in the state's interest and therefore effectively stated controlled. When underwriting an SS or SOE, the underwriter should first determine whether the SS or SOE or the transaction under consideration has an explicit sovereign guaranty. If so, the "credit" analysis would stop at the sovereign level. If not, the following questions should be answered: Does explicit or implicit support from the sovereign exist, and to what extent? What is the likelihood of default during the period that the loan is outstanding? The analysis of an SS may prove a bit more challenging because financial information on a state, province, or municipality located in an emerging market is sometimes difficult to obtain.

More specifically, for an SS, the financial indicators of concern are whether it is running a budget surplus or deficit and for how long, does it have an operating surplus or deficit, and finally, how does its interest expense compare to its revenues? The SS debt structure is another aspect to carefully consider, as is its per capita debt, particularly as compared to similar SSs; the proportion of foreign to local currency debt; and finally, its debt profile. The underwriter also considers the SS's economic fundamentals: its ability to raise its own revenues compared to its dependency on intergovernmental transfers, the local economic base, the soundness of the local infrastructure, and the management of the budgetary process (efficiently or subject to political influences or corruption). The overall relationship with the sovereign as well as its importance to the overall political system should be considered.

Underwriting an SOE may be a bit more straightforward, provided that audited financial statements are available. In that case, a credit assessment of the obligor would be the underwriter's first step. In addition to the usual financial performance indicators, a careful review of the management is in order. The management of SOEs can be subject to government whim. Chances are good that if the financial statement analysis reveals a strong commercial company, the management is professional rather than politically based. If audited financials are not available, the transaction can still be considered but will require using more of the art of underwriting rather than the science. In particular, the underwriter assesses government support for the SOE, its access to foreign exchange, and the degree to which the SOE plays a vital role in the overall functioning of the economy. Last, an underwriter assesses the SOE's position in the global marketplace.

Given recent experience, underwriters should be wary of relying upon implicit support of the SOE by the sovereign government. Even comfort letters should be viewed skeptically. Although the global financial crisis was an unprecedented event requiring governments to take extreme action, some have learned the hard way that when under extreme pressure, anything but an explicit guaranty will not get the lender very far. A few case examples follow.

Underwriting SSs and SOEs has unique challenges—in large part because of a lack of information—but one can still conduct enough due diligence to determine that a risk is acceptable. The underwriter must ultimately decide if it has enough information in light of the size of the transaction, an overall assessment of the country in which it is located, the tenor of the transaction, and the perceived strength of sovereign support. Ultimately, each transaction is unique and requires varying levels of due diligence, structuring, and risk mitigation.

Key Considerations

SOEs and SSs present several challenges which have implications for both the underwriting and contract preparation. An underwriter must consider the following factors before underwriting a risk for SSs and SOEs.

Calling on the Guaranty
Even with an explicit guaranty, the underwriter needs to consider the willingness of the insured lender to call on that guaranty. If the guaranty was critical to insuring the risk, the policy should clearly state that the covered loss is the nonpayment of a call on the guaranty following the nonpayment of the loan. Specifying the "double-trigger" in the policy makes clear that the underwriter intends to cover the sovereign's payment risk only rather than that of the SS or SOE. Even with the explicit policy wording, a lender in certain cases may be reluctant to call on a guaranty if the lender expects the sovereign to default on the guaranty as well. This situation could be caused by cross-defaults with other lenders (particularly official lenders) contained in the loan agreement. If the policy is clearly drafted, the lender will understand the effect of this decision on the ability to recover under the policy.

Basel II and III
With the implementation of Basel II requirements, many underwriters were approached to modify their policies to enable the lenders to maximize the support of the policies with respect to reserving. Several brokers also attempted to draft and market a Basel II–compliant nonhonoring policy. The challenge for the underwriter is that although the Basel Committee on Banking Supervision set standards in 2002, the various bank supervisors in each country have to interpret how those requirements are implemented. This variation, in addition to the differing speed with which each country implemented the requirements, made developing a Basel II–compliant policy virtually impossible for an underwriter. As with any request for policy modifications, underwriters have

attempted to accommodate these requests while keeping within the principle of insurance (a contingent obligation to pay) and the individual risk appetite. The vast majority of the requested changes related to actions or outcomes that are within the insured lender's control.

Basel III recommendations have been released, although the requirements will be phased in over eight years. As with Basel II, each banking regulator will have to interpret how the banks under its control must implement the new recommendations. Along with other forms of lending, the potential exists for a significant effect on lending to emerging market borrowers.

Recoveries

Recoveries play a key role in any underwriting decision. When an underwriter agrees to accept a risk, it is making an educated bet that no losses will occur on the policy. However, equally important is the determination that in the event a loss is paid, the underwriter will recover amounts paid through subrogation. In many cases, these recovery efforts involve rescheduling. After rescheduling, the underwriter can decide to sell the debt or to wait for the loan to be repaid over time.

Privatization

When offering coverage on an SOE, the underwriter and the insured need to consider what happens to the coverage in the event of a privatization. Several years ago, the approach was to include an endorsement agreeing to, in effect, renegotiate the policy to convert the coverage to currency inconvertibility and expropriation. As insureds have demanded more certainty in their coverage, the strategy of addressing the privatization "when and if it happens" is no longer acceptable. The underwriter needs to make its own assessment of the likelihood of a privatization during the policy tenor and include that factor as part of its risk appetite.

Case Examples

The three entities principally involved in cross-border sovereign debt restructurings are the IMF, the Paris Club, and the London Club. The IMF has extensive experience, given that many of the distressed countries are recipients of World Bank funding. When invited, the IMF arrives in the country with a team of economists for a period of time to assess the level and composition of debt and the economic and financial risk factors and to provide recommendations on what policy changes could be implemented to alleviate the situation.

Once the IMF has given a "reorganization plan," the country can then approach the representatives of the creditor countries, also collectively known as the "Paris Club," to negotiate a restructuring. This Paris-based forum of representatives from finance ministries and treasury departments of member countries of the Organisation for Economic Co-operation and Development meets several times a year. For a country's sovereign debt to be restructured, the proposal must receive unanimous consent from all creditor governments involved in the program. The Paris Club can agree to a standstill on debt service payments for obligations that are generally greater than one year that would fall due during a specific period of time (consolidation period). The creditor countries generally do not restructure previously rescheduled debt and avoid providing new senior financing during the standstill. The IMF can and often does, however, provide senior financing to the country while the existing debt is being restructured. Restructured debt brought before the Paris Club can be rolled over, written down, or both.

A country manages debt restructurings with private commercial banks through a mechanism called the London Club. Although numerous banks can be involved in a debt workout program, usually 12–15 large banks take the lead to negotiate with the debtor. The participant banks can, like the IMF, choose to provide bridge financing to the country during the debt restructuring process. The ultimate debt restructuring program agreed upon generally requires approval of the banks holding 90–95 percent of the exposure. Because one may have to deal with many creditor banks, a minority of banks can drag the process out over many years. The terms of the restructuring can involve a rollover as well as varying degrees of write-offs (Radelet 1999, 6–9).

Of the numerous examples of SS debt crises, a few are worth mentioning. Keeping in mind the context in which these crises came about is helpful—cascading effects resulting from a global economic depression, internal destabilization (fraud in sector, governance issues, and so on), or a combination of both. The cases are the 2005 restructuring of sovereign debt for the Dominican Republic, Dubai World in the late fall of 2009, Tema oil refinery in Ghana in 2008, and the current concern of Vinashin in Vietnam.

Dominican Republic

The Dominican Republic began to undergo a financial crisis when it had to bail out the country's second-largest private bank in 2003 after the bank revealed fraudulent accounting practices. As the country began to experience a run on other banks, the central bank injected liquidity into the monetary system, which had the perverse effect of triggering a currency devaluation because of the lack of sterilization of the increased money supply. This exacerbated the country's difficulty in meeting its sovereign debt repayments. The increase in fuel prices further contributed to the economic decline.

Finance officials began working with the IMF in rescheduling multilateral and Paris Club debt. The country was able to renegotiate arrears since 2003 and maturities of US$193 million falling in 2004. Concurrently, the Dominican Republic negotiated rescheduling of its private external debt with private creditors and international commercial banks. With private creditors, the government was able to exchange two international bonds, one of US$500 million maturing in 2005 and another of US$600 million maturing in 2013, to extend the terms five additional years with temporary capitalization of interest payments. With the London Club, the Dominican Republic was able to reschedule US$198 million with principal payments expected in 2005 and 2006 for a two-year grace period with semi-annual amortizations resuming in mid-2007. Having restructured its London Club debt, the Dominican Republic was able to sign a second agreement with the Paris Club, restructuring another US$137 million expected to mature in 2005. The rescheduling was perceived as being mostly preventive because the country was current on servicing its external debt. In total, the country rescheduled approximately US$1.6 billion over 18 months (Díaz-Cassou, Erce-Domínguez, and Vázquez-Zamora 2008, 24–28) with less than 1 percent net present value loss to all private creditors through the restructurings.

Dubai World

In 2009, the United Arab Emirates experienced a slowdown in growth as a result of the financial crisis, the decline in oil prices, and the dramatic cooling of the overheated property market. The banking system in particular took a hit as asset quality deteriorated and loans began to underperform. Dubai World, the giant, government-owned investment conglomerate, manages a portfolio of businesses and projects for the Dubai government, spanning development, hospitality, investment, financial services, commodities, marine services, and ports and free zones. In late November, Dubai World, too, succumbed to the global contagion and announced that it would put a six-month standstill on payments and that it needed to restructure part of its US$26 billion debt (Wearden 2009). The announcement roiled bond and equity markets around the world with certificates of deposit for Dubai debt doubling to over 600 basis points in three days. Investors began to take aim at the risk of default in other countries throughout the region. Many global banks such as Barclays, Royal Bank of Scotland (RBS), and Deutsche Bank were significantly exposed to the region and lost billions of dollars overnight.

The Dubai government began with the position that it refused to guarantee the SOE's debts of some US$59 billion. "Creditors need to take part of the responsibility for their decision to lend to the companies… the company is not guaranteed by the [Dubai] government," according to the director general of Dubai's department of finance (Teather 2009). However, the central bank of the United Arab Emirates immediately made funds available to banks in the region to allay widespread concerns about liquidity problems.

As Dubai World's credit ratings deteriorated, so did those of many other SOEs in the emirate. Moody's long-term FC (foreign currency) ratings for Dubai fell seven notches from A1 in August 2009 to Baa2 by the end of November and have been sitting at Ba1 (down another two notches) since April 2010. By the end of December 2010, six more SOEs fell to junk-bond status and began to default on their own debts. Nakheel, the real estate firm, asked for a halt in its US$3.5 billion *sukuk* (Islamic financial certificate) due December

14, 2009, because of a dramatic loss in its profits resulting from write-downs in its real estate portfolio and lower sales (Moya 2009). Not until December 14 did Dubai World make payments to creditors, thanks to a US$10 billion lifeline from Abu Dhabi to Dubai. The central bank of the United Arab Emirates and the government of Abu Dhabi came to the strong support of Dubai to assure investors that banks would not fail and the crisis would be contained. While restructuring negotiations were going on through the spring, the government of Dubai injected another US$9.5 billion to support repayment of Nakheel's bonds and interest payments for other SOEs.

In September 2010, Dubai World announced a 99 percent acceptance rate of the final terms of its debt restructuring plan with bank creditors (London Club). The restructured debt comes to US$24.9 billion, of which US$14.4 billion goes to creditor banks and the remainder to the Dubai government. The terms of the restructuring agreement are to convert the debt into a five-year tranche and an eight-year tranche (Zawya.com 2010).

Tema Oil Refinery

The Tema Oil Refinery (TOR) was established in Ghana in 1963 with a 25,000-barrel capacity. Over time, the refinery failed to keep pace with global demand, and finally after more than 30 years, the government decided to upgrade the facility to increase the barrel capacity to 45,000 and to improve efficiency with a catalytic converter. A consortium from the Republic of Korea, led by the energy subsidiary of Samsung and the infrastructure company Sunkyong, were contracted to manage the expansion in two phases between 1996 and 2002, which cost more than 210 million Ghanaian cedis (¢). The consortium also had ¢110 million in open letters of credit with banks to import crude oil. With high interest rates on its maturing loans, liabilities were approximately ¢470 million in 2003. In 2004, the government decided to "absorb" ¢320 million in the form of cash defrayments and in financing of ¢240 million in dollarized bonds, leaving ¢150 million on the books (Simons and Cudjoe 2009).

By December 2008, TOR had accumulated more than C598 million in outstanding debt with Ghana Commercial Bank (GCB), mostly in the form of open letters of credit. The refinery began to experience crude delivery payments because of its weak financial situation in February 2009. The high cost of imported fuel and the low output costs caused by government price restrictions made the refinery hugely unprofitable and a significant credit concern to lenders. The government had to negotiate contracts with other African countries to maintain the supply of crude oil, given the refinery's difficult financial position.

In September 2009, the government appointed Ecobank Development Corporation and Ecobank Ghana as transaction advisers to determine the actual TOR debt and raise US$600 million to help settle part of the debt and restructure the rest of TOR's balance sheet (Think Ghana 2010). If one takes into account payments in arrears and accrued interest payments, the debt with GCB swelled to C848 million by March 2010. The government paid C445 million to help reduce TOR's outstanding loans with GCB, which also improved the financial standing of the bank and allowed it to write additional letters of credit for the refinery (GNA 2010). Currently, the government plans to raise more bonds to finance the rest of the debt. The changes in the Ghanaian government have complicated the ability to successfully restructure TOR's debt.

Vinashin

Vinashin, the Vietnam Shipbuilding Industry Group, was established in 1972 to develop the country's shipbuilding industry. It is one of the largest SOEs with more than 39 shipyards employing more than 70,000 people throughout the country. The company provides 70–80 percent of domestic shipbuilding capacity and began receiving international orders in 2000. The company had signed contracts worth more than US$12 billion through 2009 but lost many contracts (approximately US$8 billion) because of cancellations. These cancellations occurred as Vinashin began to miss certain contractual milestones.

Vinashin's accumulated debts were approximately US$4.5 billion, while total asset worth was only US$5.4 billion (through June 2010). The company was also the sole recipient of proceeds from a US$750 million Vietnam bond issue in October 2005, which Vinashin is obligated to repay by 2012. Through a combination of internal mismanagement of funds; a business strategy resulting in 169 subsidiaries, many unrelated to the core objective; and a deteriorating economic environment, the company found itself at the brink of bankruptcy in midsummer 2010 (Ngo Khac Le 2010). Following investigations into mismanagement of the SOE, the government set up a committee to oversee restructuring of the group. Other SOEs will take over many projects and subsidiaries. The government has also reorganized the group's debt among other SOEs. Vinashin's most significant debt obligations are loans from local banks and salaries to workers. The State Bank of Vietnam has ordered domestic commercial banks to suspend all payments on Vinashin debt until 2013.

With regard to the company's foreign debt obligations, Credit Suisse placed a US$600 million facility in 2006 that was mostly issued through foreign creditors. Deutsche Bank also issued a US$187 million corporate bond in 2007 (Steinglass 2010). Vinashin finished repaying its US$25 million loan to Natixis Bank at the end of September 2010 and plans to use US$130 million of government funds to complete several shipbuilding orders that will allow it to further pay down its debt (Viet Nam Business News 2010). Another US$60 million payment of principal on Credit Suisse loans was due December 2010.

These case studies demonstrate that governments have taken a variety of actions in response to severe economic crisis. Each government considers its maneuvering room as well as the long-term effect on its access to external sources of financing that may result from any strategy it pursues.

CHAPTER 7

Sovereign Risk and Political Risk: New Challenges from a Financial Institution's Perspective

Catherine Aubert

This chapter addresses the perspective of a user of policies covering the nonhonoring of sovereign risks, the merits of the coverage, and the issues Société Générale (SG) has faced. It also comments on the potential challenges the industry should be considering going forward.

This is not a scholarly chapter. It is based on experience as head of trade credit and political risks insurance at SG in charge of the relationships with the private insurance market (Lloyd's and the company market), and therefore, the main focus is the private insurance market.

SG values the political risk insurance (PRI) market as a whole. SG has been extensively using the products offered by export credit agencies (ECAs) for many years now and has lately intensified relationships with multilateral agencies.

Given the title of the panel session—"Sovereign Risk and Political Risk: New Challenges"—first defining what these concepts mean and outlining the difference in terminology used by insurers and banks would be useful. The chapter then examines the types of cover used by banks and the benefits of these strategies. Last, it expands the subject to types of risks other than political and sovereign risks that reflect a change in banks' needs. In addressing these new challenges, the chapter examines the evolution of banks' needs and how the private market should respond.

What Do We Mean by Sovereign and Political Risks?

First, one should point out that banks do not use the terms *sovereign risks* and *political risks*. Banks use the concepts of *country risk* and *credit risk*. In the banking environment, transactions are subject to country risks whenever their successful completion is linked to the political, economic, social, or financial situation in the country where the debtor is located. Country risk occurs through two major types of risk: (a) political risk (nontransfer, nationalization, expropriation, civil war, war, and so on) and (b) economic and financing risk, which can be split between commercial risk and sovereign risk. The concepts of country risk and credit risk exclude market and operational risks, which this chapter does not discuss.

"Political Risk" Has No Common Understanding or Standard Definition

In the context of this chapter, *political risk* is the risk that a private obligor will default on its obligations because of political risks such as expropriation, currency inconvertibility and nontransfer, political violence, breach of contract by the host government, and nonhonoring of sovereign obligations. *Sovereign risk* is the risk that a government will default on its financial obligations as a borrower or as a guarantor.

If one switches to insurance terminology from Lloyd's, sovereign risk (as well as state-owned enterprises) is covered under contract frustration (CF) policies and political risk is covered under the heading of lenders PRI cover. Another type of policy covers the nonpayment of private obligors under structured credit insurance or trade credit insurance (risk code: CR).

In fact, banks do not differentiate by type of obligor (sovereign, public, or private) but by the extent of the cover. The distinction banks make is between *comprehensive cover* (nonpayment for any reason whatsoever) and *political risks–only cover* (a named political perils policy in which commercial risk is excluded).

This differentiation between comprehensive and political risks–only cover is reflected in the banks' internal treatment of these two covers in respect of risk-weighted assets and risk relief—with a more favorable treatment for comprehensive covers. Comprehensive cover is a "risk transfer mechanism," whereas political risks–only cover is a "risk mitigant."

Banks Prefer Comprehensive Covers

Comprehensive cover represents the bulk of cover bought by banks. It is simpler to enforce because the insured is required to prove only that the loss is caused by the failure of the borrower (or guarantor) to pay in accordance with the finance documents, whereas under a *lenders cover,* the bank must prove that the loss is caused (sometimes solely and directly) by one of the insured events.

Banks fear potential conflicts in the interpretation of the policy terms in a claim situation for various reasons. Contrary to common belief, political risk policies are not country risk policies. They cover only named political perils. In addition, for such a policy to be triggered, the event causing the loss must be exactly reflected in the policy wording. Some events can be relatively easy to prove, such as currency inconvertibility or nontransfer, but the expropriation peril, for example, could easily be a cause for debate. Another major cause for potential dispute is the determinination whether the proximate cause of loss is of a commercial or a political risk nature (as defined under the policy terms). In reality, the cause of loss may involve a combination of both.

Banks do not want to take the risk that lenders cover will not respond because nonresponse would jeopardize all the work done over the years to convince bank management and risk departments that insurance works. Banks learned at their expense from the Argentine crisis that lenders' PRI policies were difficult to enforce, and the damage caused to the insurance market globally took a few years to be repaired. When comprehensive cover is available even at a higher price, banks will buy it.

That being said, comprehensive cover is not always available, notably for long tenors or project finance structures; lenders cover can then still be useful. Insurers should develop a product focused on country risks (and not only named political risks) that will cover nonpayment for any reason except commercial risk. The scope of this product would be halfway between a comprehensive cover and a lenders form. The potential dispute on the nature (commercial or political) of the cause of loss would remain but not the question about the definition of political risks.

Diversity Is an Asset in Banks' Relationships with the PRI Market

Most banks work with the PRI market as a whole to take advantage of the specific merits of each type of provider: ECAs, multilaterals, and private market. For instance, ECA and multilateral support remains critical for longer tenors and on large deals. They enable banks to attract private capacity on difficult emerging countries because ECAs' and multilaterals' clout may help avoid a default situation.

The private market is now a key partner for banks, and banks have become the private market's main buyers. The bulk of insurance bought by banks is on a comprehensive cover basis. SG has been using this market for more than 10 years, and its use has grown dramatically over the past few years.

Reasons for Banks to Use Private Insurance

Portfolio management on the loans banks hold to maturity is the main driver for using private insurance. Insurance enables banks to mitigate country and obligor limits. It also has a positive effect on risk-weighted assets. In addition, insurance enables banks to take bigger participations without the client knowing that the bank is off-loading part of the risk because the purchase is confidential. An additional advantage is that insurers are not competitors with banks in this field, so sharing a client relationship or expertise on highly structured deals has no downside.

Private insurance competes with other risk transfer mechanisms. The SG Trade Credit and Political Risks Insurance team is part of the syndication department. This positioning reflects that insurance (comprehensive cover) is now established as one of the distribution tools alongside loan syndication, secondary sales, credit default swaps, and so on. On each transaction, business lines assess the respective merits of each distribution tool. Private insurance is thus in competition with other risk transfer mechanisms and must maintain its key advantages.

Demand for Insurance Has Changed

Insurance requests on sovereign risks cover have decreased while they have increased on private obligors. When banks began to work with the private insurance market more than 10 years ago, they were insuring mostly risks on sovereign or public obligors on export finance transactions. Today the bulk of the requests are on private obligors and stem from various departments within banks.

This trend can be explained by the following events. After the Russian and Asian crisis in the late 1990s, banks had to face dramatic country limit restrictions. These constraints have now globally eased except on certain countries. Banks also faced a privatization trend and, consequently, a growing need for financing from private obligors. Lately, the recent crisis has led to a widening of ECA activity with fewer requests for insurance on commercial loans linked to buyer credits.

Demand exists for sovereign risk insurance but not at the level seen in the past. However, a need for cover still exists in many of the least-developed countries on sovereign lending transactions and on nonhonoring of sovereign obligations in project finance deals. The demand may also increase on industrial countries where sovereign risk has deteriorated and on export finance deals if commercial loan pricing continues to decrease, because ECA loans will become more expensive.

Demand for Nonemerging Markets and Nontrade-Related Deals Has Increased

The major lesson banks have learned from the 2008 financial crisis is that industrial countries are also exposed to economic cycles and crises, and that in the current crisis, they have been even more affected than emerging markets. Emerging markets are recovering quickly and have driven international trade lately. The bipolar model of emerging countries ("risky") versus the developed countries ("nonrisky") is probably behind us.

The other trend is a growing demand to cover risks on private obligors and on nontrade-related transactions. Banks struggle with the fact that insurers and reinsurers view trade-related deals as less risky than nontrade-related ones. Except for some insurers outside of Lloyd's and those having limited or no reinsurance constraints, the first question insurers ask themselves before underwriting a deal is whether it is trade related and whether it is secured.

Banks do not analyze deals this way. At the end of the day, banks take a credit risk. Banks analyze the risk of the obligor together with the structure. Structures are intended to enable the bank to be in a better bargaining position in a restructuring process. This is what has happened in a number of cases.

The payment track record of banks on nontrade-related deals is as good as on trade-related ones globally. In addition, the recent crisis and the surge of credit claims has shown that, contrary to insurers' perceptions, recovery rates on private obligors can be substantial.

Banks Expect and Need the Long-term Presence of Insurers in the PRI Market and Stability in Insurers' Ratings

The opportunistic nature of private insurers and the fact that trade credit and PRI represent only a small share of the insurers' premium volume raise issues regarding the long-term involvement of some of the players. A number of insurance companies have ceased their activities over the past few years, Chubb among them recently. This type of event is extremely detrimental for banks' business. Banks want to work with long-term partners, not with opportunistic partners who will not assist the banks in situations where their approval is required in case of waivers or restructurings. Insurers in a run-off period will obviously have a different agenda and may not take a long-term view on recoveries, for example. They will not have the same commercial stance as ongoing insurers.

Trade credit and PRI may not be a core business for some of the private market insurers, and banks will always be exposed to the risk of an insurer exiting the market. Banks would not have the same fears with ECAs and multilaterals.

The Insurance Market Should Innovate and Adapt to New Trends

Private market insurance capacity is at an all time high, and plenty of capacity is available for sovereign and public obligations in most cases. The Multilateral Investment Guarantee Agency has lately expanded its scope of cover by including nonhonoring of sovereign obligations. But a lack of capacity exists for credit, especially for periods over three years and for nontrade-related deals. The requirement from insurers for a cross-border element is also outdated.

Insurers should be able to offer new products in response to evolving customer needs with the support of their reinsurers.

Risk-weighted Asset Constraint Is Less of an Issue Today, Whereas Liquidity Constraints Are of Paramount Importance

Premium rates are often quoted on the basis of the gross margin. The problem banks face is the increased cost of liquidity they have to bear, which reduces their net remuneration. Banks would therefore like insurers to show flexibility in their pricing and take into account the liquidity costs by quoting on the basis of the net margin. Banks are also looking for funded risk participations, which are unfortunately not the case with insurance covers.

The Basel III Effect on PRI Is Still Unknown

The consequences of Basel III implementation on the use of the PRI market by banks cannot yet be gauged. However, banks fear that collateral and guarantees will be less favorably treated than under Basel II.

Know Your Customer

The insurer must have a good understanding of the bank's expertise in the type of financings and countries in which it operates, its experience in dealing with difficult cases, and its track record in dealing with the private market.

The existence of a centralized trade credit and PRI department within a bank having a long presence in this class of business is a key advantage for insurers. Insurers benefit from a sole entry point and can gain additional comfort because the insurance team will endeavor to maintain long-term relationships with insurers and ensure a win-win situation for both parties. Conversely, if the transaction parties deal directly with insurers, a risk exists that they would take an opportunistic approach to get the most out of their deal.

Anti-selection Should Not Be a Concern

Insurers should not worry about anti-selection from regular buyers of the product for the following reasons. Deals that are shown to the market have to pass the same internal filters (through the risk department), and they will not be validated only because of support from a PRI provider. The bank must be comfortable with the underlying risk in the first place before looking for any risk mitigant or distribution tool.

The PRI market's products really suit only commercial banking activity in which loans are held to maturity. As a result, the deal (and not the uninsured part only) is still on the bank's books, as are the operational risks that go with it. Thus, banks have skin in the game.

In addition, a bank's objective is to maintain a strong relationship with its clients and support them through difficult times. During the crisis, SG has taken the option of restructuring deals when possible rather than calling on the insurance policies. Last, banks would soon bring the insurance market to its knees if they were just filling the market with bad risks. This is definitely not in the banks' interest. Like other buyers of insurance, banks do not want to have claims, but where claims arise, banks do want them settled cleanly and quickly.

Who Before What?

"Who" you insure is more important than "what" you insure, and insurers have learned this lesson during the crisis. Understanding the insured must be as important (or even more important) as understanding the deal itself. Trust, transparency, and ongoing communication between the two parties are paramount.

Global Client Relationship Concept

An alignment of interests definitely exists between banks and insurers, and after many years of working together, they now have a good understanding of each other's practices. They also have mutual respect.

As the relationship develops, a bank moves from covering occasional transactions to providing a sustainable deal flow to the market. Insurers must be partners and try to cover banks' needs (for example, on nontrade-related deals on private obligors) once they have gained comfort with the way their insured operates. Insurers must select a few banks with which they wish to develop a global relationship approach.

In a nutshell, what major banks are looking for at the end of the day is the same type of relationship that an insurer seeks with its reinsurers. Indeed, what the PRI market provides to banks is a form of facultative reinsurance, and the insurance market should be comfortable with this because it reflects the nature of the insurance business.

Conclusion

The supply for coverage of nonhonoring of sovereign obligations currently meets banks' overall demand, except on long tenors and on the most difficult emerging countries.

Significant developments on the demand side have increased requests for insurance cover on private obligors, on nontrade-related transactions, and in nonemerging countries.

Insurers should try to adapt to banks' needs. Instead of selecting the type of deals they wish to insure (for example, export finance and oil commodity business), insurers should select the insured first and provide a full service to the extent possible. Banks are looking for a "global client relationship" approach and not for an opportunistic one.

The resilience of the insurance market in terms of financial strength and the recent good track record have led to more confidence in the private market by banks' management and risk departments. Higher use by banks of the PRI market can be anticipated, should insurers and reinsurers maintain their support on sovereign and political risks, especially on long tenors and on risky countries. Insurers should also expand their scope on other types of risks, such as credit risk, nontrade-related business, and nonemerging country covers.

Last, because diversity is an asset, banks will continue to use all PRI providers, and cooperation between these markets will certainly increase over the next few years.

CHAPTER 8

Looking Back and Looking Forward: The Future of the Political Risk Insurance Industry

Gerald T. West and Julie Martin

Introduction

In an extended metaphor, Warren Buffett likened writing certain kinds of insurance to driving down a mountain road with a mud-covered windshield that hindered the driver from looking forward, so that steering was accomplished by using the rearview mirror. This metaphor captures a phenomenon that is familiar to most political risk investment insurers writing longer-term coverages. Future political perils appear to be quite opaque as to their occurrence, magnitude, and timing, and looking backward is one of the few useful guides about how best to go forward.

Notwithstanding muddy windshields, one must acknowledge that Buffett's insurance businesses (and most political risk insurers) have been exceptionally successful for many years. Buffet's insurance successes have been attributed to a combination of disciplined underwriting, prudent investment, and astute management.

But to what extent was the success of political risk investment insurers attributable to disciplined underwriting, prudent investment, and astute management, or to simple good fortune? How well do members of the political risk investment insurance industry see into the future and manage accordingly? These are not easy questions to address. Fortunately, about 90 papers are included in the six books published in the past 12 years in the aftermath of the previous six symposia on political risk management hosted by the Multilateral Investment Guarantee Agency (MIGA) and Georgetown University. Some of these papers address technical and operational issues or analyze current issues; others are full of various forecasts, nuanced prognostications, trend identifications, warnings, and cautions. In the aggregate, these papers constitute a rich record of what was foreseen for the political risk investment insurance industry.

Although each paper was a product of the particular circumstances extant at the time and reflected the unique perspective of each author, one can selectively reexamine and learn from these papers while seeking to look forward from 2010.

Most forecasts, like mosaics, are best viewed from a distance. For this reason, forecasts that were offered in papers presented at the 2008 MIGA-Georgetown Political Risk Management Symposium will not be addressed. Structurally, this paper is divided into four parts.

Section I looks back over the forecasts offered at the first three symposia (1997, 2000, and 2002) regarding where the political risk investment insurance industry was thought to be going. Although individual elements in these forecasts will be examined, *the larger perspective will be the focus*. In terms of format, each author's "vision" will be succinctly summarized, followed by summary commentary and reflections.

Section II examines three "macro" forecasts made by the following authors in *International Political Risk Management: Looking to the Future* (Moran and West 2005), the book encompassing the 2004 symposium: Clive Tobin, then CEO (chief executive officer) of XL Insurance, who wrote "The Future of the International Political Risk Insurance Industry"; Toby Heppel, then of FirstCity Partnership, who wrote "Perspectives on Public-Private Relationships in Political Risk Insurance"; and Gerald West and Kristopher Hamel of MIGA, who wrote "Whither the Political Risk Insurance Industry?"

Section III examines the specific group of forecasts and analyses produced by a panel at the 2006 symposium titled "The International Political Risk Insurance Industry in 2010." In that panel, three industry experts and an investor opined about the state of the industry in 2010. Because 2010 has occured, it is appropriate to pay special attention to those papers. Fortunately, the MIGA-Georgetown Political Risk Management Symposium VII includes the chairperson and two members of that original panel—to modestly discuss their previous insights, to explain away any shortcomings, and to further reflect on their earlier thoughts (and perhaps to boldly look forward once again to the year 2015).

Section IV, in view of the changing contexts in which the political risk investment insurance industry was operating in the past, is informed by an awareness of the accuracies and inaccuracies of past forecasts. Acknowledging the challenging environment of the future, it argues that looking forward is best approached with humility, with broad brushstrokes, and with consideration for possible actions for the political risk investment insurance industry.

Looking Back at Early Forecasts of the Future of the Private Risk Investment Insurance Industry

As noted in the introduction, this section attempts to broadly characterize the forecasts made during the first three symposia. It is convenient to divide these forecasts into two chronological periods.

The Late 1990s: The Era of Optimism

The first MIGA-Georgetown symposium (1997) was held during a period of general optimism. It is useful to recall the general international investment milieu at the time. Between 1990 and 1997, private capital flows to developing countries and emerging markets increased fivefold to US$256 billion with the bulk of that being in the form of foreign direct investment (FDI). Fears of expropriation that had dominated investors' concerns in the 1960s, 1970s, and 1980s were clearly on the wane. One presenter at the first symposium, Sandy Marwick of Control Risks, observed that free markets had increasingly taken root in the developing world and "ideology has given way to pragmatism"; moreover, democracy had spread and authoritarian military regimes and one-party states "stood out as notable exceptions" (Marwick 1998). The *World Investment Report 1997* (UN 1997) noted that between 1990 and 1997, some 65 countries made 575 positive changes in the regulations affecting foreign direct investors. Many countries began to create investment promotion agencies to attract FDI, dismantling onerous investment screening procedures, and markedly reducing rhetorical attacks on the evils of capitalism.

The opening of Eastern Europe to foreign private investors, the privatization phenomenon in many countries, and the rise of project finance, especially in infrastructure and energy, all combined with other favorable factors to give rise to barely restrained investor euphoria. There were some voices of restraint, however, noting that the old political risks had not entirely disappeared and that new risks were emerging. In this respect, Lou Wells (1998) noted the weaknesses of the governance structures in many countries, the weak regulatory entities, and the absence of real protection of intellectual property rights. Marwick (1998) added to this list of new risks the inadequacies of some legal systems, corruption, organized crime, nongovernmental organization scrutiny of investors, and sanctions and embargoes. But by and large, there was a pervasive optimism among investors; the prospective returns from investing in developing and emerging markets seemed to far outweigh any possible risks.

The New Optimism and the Political Risk Insurance Industry

While the flows of foreign direct investment were surging in the 1990s, the collective levels of Berne Union investment insurance issued rose modestly from about US$2.5 billion in 1990 to US$12 billion in 2000. However, if one examines the ratio of FDI covered by Berne Union insurers to the total flow of FDI to developing countries, there was an actual decline from about 11 percent to 5 percent—notwithstanding a slight increase in Berne Union membership (West and Martin 2001). These macro statistics, however, masked a number of other important phenomena affecting the political risk investment insurance industry.

First, there was a significant amount of risk retention (or self-insurance) by both equity and debt investors venturing into emerging markets. The end of the Cold War, the opening of scores of new countries to private investments, and the abandonment of anticapitalist rhetoric in many other countries imbued investors with great confidence that they could bear whatever few political risks might remain.

Second, some national insurers wrote very little coverage, others fluctuated widely from year to year in coverage issued, and a few remained relatively stable. The Overseas Private Investment Corporation (OPIC), which had regularly averaged US$1–2 billion of new coverage issued in the 1980s, was much more volatile in the 1990s. MIGA, which issued its first policies in 1990 (US$132 million), grew to write more than US$1.3 billion annually by 1999. Demand for MIGA coverage was large enough (relative to its capital base) in the late 1990s for MIGA to seek and successfully secure a doubling of its capital base by its member countries by 2000.

Third, a number of institutions, especially the multilateral development banks (but including some private institutions as well), began writing various kinds of guarantee policies at very attractive rates that encompassed both political and commercial risks. Although the hassle of obtaining a guarantee was often onerous and time-consuming, it was a type of risk transfer that competed with the traditional offerings of investment insurers.

Finally, the private political risk insurance industry came of age in the late 1990s. In 1990, private political risk insurers were few in number and provided limited coverage for short durations. By 1997, both the number of insurers and the volume provided had grown dramatically; these insurers included ACE, AIG (American International Group), Chubb, CIGNA, Lloyd's, Sovereign, XL, and Zurich, among others. The combination of competition and more capacity, together with very attractive loss ratios, served to fuel an extension of the industry's offerings in terms of duration, scope of risks covered, and amounts of coverage available per project. By John Salinger's (*Managing International Political Risk, T. Moran, Ed.*, 1998) estimation in 1997, there were 23 companies that underwrote political risk insurance and 43 syndicates at Lloyd's; it was theoretically possible to arrange as much as US$1 billion in coverage of a single risk. Moreover, there were growing efforts by both private and public sector insurers to work together—whether as coinsurers or reinsurers. (Because most of these private insurers were not at the time members of the Berne Union, their activities were not captured in the macrostatistics cited earlier.)

Investors did not, in this optimistic era, cease their efforts to transfer political risks to one another or to insurance or noninsurance parties. Multiple presenters at the first symposium argued that new deal structures (especially those for finance projects with limited recoursecalled for new risk management tools and that governments (of both home and host countries) should supply various kinds of new guarantees and protections to both equity and debt investors.

Linda Powers, Enron

Linda Powers, then Senior Vice President of Enron International (Powers 1998), argued at the first symposium that the need for new risk management tools was particularly acute for large energy projects facing contract frustration risks in developing and emerging country markets. Powers noted that there was a specific need for more protection for investors outside of the deal structure. In this regard, she had guarded praise for the potential of MIGA's Cooperative Underwriting Program (CUP) and guarded regret that private insurers had not been more willing to improve their contract frustration coverage. She noted that a special group in Enron's Houston headquarters was working on a finite insurance program with private insurers that would combine elements of risk transfer and risk financing. Such a hybrid risk transfer and risk financing program would provide tailored coverage for situations in which a sophisticated party feels "pretty sure" that it will not encounter a big problem—and thus does not want to pay much for protection—but does not feel confident enough to operate without any protection whatsoever.

Powers made an additional argument about the importance of bringing in new coverage providers for political risk investment insurance coverage. Noting the positive contributions that new entrants had made to the market since 1995, she argued that bringing in additional players would contribute to expanding of the extant market for political risk investment insurance coverage. Enron, she noted, was already in discussions with onshore parties (for example, local pension funds, financial institutions, and so forth) in host countries where infrastructure projects were to be located. These parties, she argued, bring de facto political risk protection beyond the actual coverage they may provide. Enron was also seeking ways for noninsurance company capital markets players to become involved in providing political risk protections (for example, catastrophe bonds modeled on those created for hurricane and earthquake exposures).

Powers further argued that in the handling of political risk, there is a need to introduce greater liquidity into the protection mechanisms used for infrastructure projects, given that the amount of political risk protection needed—and the price of such protection—can vary greatly over a project's long life. Traditional political risk protection mechanisms, however, lacked flexibility and did not allow a sponsor to move into and out of coverage. To overcome this rigidity, Powers noted, Enron was working on several possible avenues to introduce flexibility, including the use of credit derivatives (such as default swaps), the use of the Catastrophe Risk Exchange (CATEX) electronic trading forum, and the development of Enron's own two-way trading of country and political risks. Although admitting to some challenging issues that would need to be addressed before the research could come to fruition, Powers expressed optimism that credit derivatives could be developed to handle contract frustration risks.

With respect to CATEX, Powers noted that Enron was one of the early subscribers and had recently become the first party to post units of political risk for placement. She noted her excitement about CATEX's potential for trading political risk units because of the liquidity it could introduce and the way it might attract many new entrants—including capital market entitiesto the exchange.

Finally, Powers noted that Enron was working in-house on the launch of a political risk trading book—much like its large and successful gas and electricity trading books. She concluded that "Enron is quite hopeful that it will prove feasible to build a political risk trading book."

Reflections

In retrospect, it is difficult to ignore the reality that roughly four years after these forecasts were so optimistically uttered, the Enron bankruptcy became the largest bankruptcy in American history and that its downfall also brought about the dissolution of Arthur Andersen, one of the largest accountancies in the world. Inflated revenues from Enron's trading activities and the masking of debt resulted in a massive loss to shareholders (the stock price fell from US$90.00 per share in August 2000 to US$0.12 in January 2002). Widespread loss of employment (both at Enron and elsewhere) was exacerbated, in many instances, by employees' loss of their pensions (which were 62 percent invested in Enron's stock). A group of senior Enron executives were eventually convicted of various crimes.

At the time of the 1997 symposium, however, all of these events were still a few years away. But the skies over Enron's Dabhol project had already begun to darken. In retrospect, it is difficult not to read into Powers's paper a frantic search for mechanisms to avoid the unfolding imbroglio that was to engulf Dabhol's shareholders, lenders, and political risk insurers for many years.

Enron did not build a political risk trading book, and, as far as these authors are aware, CATEX did not include political risk events. Finite insurance in the political risk area has been very limited, and the relatively few transactions of which the authors are aware have occurred in combination with other perils (and have been included at a relatively low level). On the plus side, over the past dozen years, there have been new entrants into the political risk investment insurance market and traditional insurers have gradually expanded their capacity as well as their per-country and per capita limits.

It should be noted that Linda Powers left Enron shortly after the first symposium (that is, long before the infamous scandal broke) to cofound a successful venture capital firm in the biotechnology field.

Malcolm Stevens

From his many years as head of the United Kingdom's Export Credits Guarantee Department (ECGD), his service as President of the Berne Union from 1989 to 1992, and his service as Secretary General of the Berne Union from 1992 to 1998, Malcolm Stevens offered not only his paper titled "A Perspective on Political Risk Experience," but also a substantial historical perspective on the entire political risk investment insurance industry. He began his paper by iterating four general points:

1. Political risks are not a thing of the past.
2. Political risks themselves are undergoing great changes.
3. There is now (then 1997) an uncomfortably large grey area between political and commercial risks.
4. The next 10 years are unlikely to be like the last 10 years. They will be far more risky for both investors and lenders.

Subsequent to a brief historical review of why public sector entities had dominated the political risk and investment risk fields, Stevens noted that this trend had changed in the 1990s. Because of the international debt crisis of the 1980s, among other things, there was a significant disenchantment with sovereign guarantees, both from those who gave the guarantees and those who received them or regarded them as the main security for their activities. This situation led to the rapid development of project finance and, subsequently, to an increase in the need to accurately price political risk so as to make better decisions regarding who will bear the risk.

Stevens noted that there was a great deal of talk about collaboration between public and private investment insurers, but that relatively little had occurred; nonetheless, it will be a key for shaping the future of the industry. There was a growing capacity and willingness in the reinsurance industry to take on such risks, a situation that offers the possibility of breaking large transactions into relatively small packets and spreading them over a large number of underwriters—both public and private.

However, the key determinant for the future of the industry is what happens to the risks. If few problems arise, then investors will want little or no insurance and demand will fall, as will supply. If, however, serious problems and large claims abound, then the effects on private insurers and reinsurers could be swift and significant. Although Stevens concurred with the belief that massive "old-style expropriation" is unlikely to reoccur, he asserted that governmental "squeezing" of investors will likely grow. Whether this will be seen as creeping expropriation will be an important question.

For many official insurers, the "mandates" from their governments are likely to be under strain. If official insurers are reduced to being "insurers of last resort," then they will have great difficulty breaking even because they need a spread of risks. So the public sector entities will be challenged to both cooperate and compete with private underwriters. There will be a great need to forge shared views on many matters—including claims and salvage issues.

Cooperation must, in Stevens's view, be based on continuing relationships—not just a withdrawal of the public insurer when a private insurer appears. If official insurers simply withdrew because other insurers were prepared to write the business, a number of consequences would follow:

1. Customer choice would disappear or be reduced.
2. Official insurers would have little or no spread of risk and a horrible concentration of risk and exposure.
3. Starved of premium income, official insurers would lack the income to keep a basic infrastructure of staff members and expertise in place. (This situation would not easily or quickly be recreated.)

Finally, Stevens noted that he did not agree with the popular view that the more insurers or lenders that are involved in a particular case the better.

He observed that large numbers of insurers and lenders inevitably mean that a complexity of almost geometric proportions would exist. In the event of problems, he argued, it will be very difficult to keep the creditors together and resolve the issues.

Reflections

From the vantage point of 2010, it is clear that Stevens was prescient in a number of areas. Political risks have not become a thing of the past and have continued to evolve. Stevens, along with many other industry observers at the time, held a commonly shared view that "outright" nationalizations were a thing of the past, but Hugo Chavez, Rafael Morales, and Evo Correa have proven that view wrong. Stevens was correct in envisaging that political risks would undergo changes—evident in the growth of terrorism and the increase in "creeping" expropriation. Countries that privatized much of their infrastructure without the proper regulatory and financing infrastructure in place were likely to try to reclaim the infrastructure when times grew more difficult, when the infrastructure did not work, or when it was politically expedient to do so. In addition, there were "inadvertent" expropriations such as occurred in some of the Argentine cases.

Stevens's point regarding the gray area between political and commercial risks has also proven accurate. Underwriters still struggle with how to separate the two types of risks, particularly when the purchaser is a government entity. Nonetheless, many underwriters for political risk investment insurance leapt into covering commercial risks directly without looking as thoroughly as they should have. This situation has led to some of the most significant claims (about US$2 billion) paid by insurers.

Stevens also noted the strain on the government agency mandates. Although these authors are not as familiar with every public agency outside of North America, certainly OPIC, Export Development Cananda (EDC), and MIGA have struggled to find their appropriate roles in different ways. The OPIC of the mid-1990s did not resemble the OPIC of a decade later. (In one recent year, OPIC supported 12 projects, the largest of which was US$5 million; in the mid-1990s, the number of projects exceeded 150 and many of those projects were exceeded US$50 million.) Stevens's observations and forecasts about the consequences remain relevant today.

Stevens reminded us that the political risk investment insurance business is characterized by adverse selection. "Safe" investments in "good" countries do not seek insurance coverage. Hence, it is difficult for insurers and reinsurers—either public or private—to build a book of business with a good spread across sectors and countries. Working out the modalities of both cooperating and competing with other insurers has been and continues to be an ongoing challenge for the industry.

John Salinger

Immediately following Malcolm Stevens, John Salinger offered a few succinct predictions about the future of the private political risk investment market:

1. Political risk is not a diminishing threat. To the extent that projects go forward, demand for coverage will increase.
2. There will continue to be downward pressure on rates; as new capacity rolls in, rates will remain soft.
3. Some markets will explore new areas of coverage, including breach of contract performance and guarantees of performance by subsovereign entities. Demand for such coverages will be strong.

Reflections

Salinger was reasonably accurate in his forecasts. Demand for political risk investment insurance coverage thereafter increased broadly for private insurers and selectively for some public insurers. However, demand for such coverage slowed as the number of private infrastructure projects dropped off and some covered projects began to have problems. Demand also shifted from the public market to the private market as it became a more viable option in terms of tenor and limits. New capacity entered the markets as the private insurers were able almost continually to expand their limits per project until the events of September 11, 2001, but rates remained soft for a few years. After September 11, new capacity entered the terrorism market, which overlapped, to some extent, with the political risk investment insurance market. Breach of contract coverage, also known as arbitration award default or contract frustration, was as much in demand for infrastructure and natural resources projects as it had been during the 1990s, and it became somewhat more mainstream until claims began to occur. Subsovereign coverage did expand, but it remained somewhat limited as insurers continued to struggle to assess the credit risk of these entities.

The 2000 Symposium: The New Realism

The second MIGA-Georgetown symposium was held in April 2000 and was dominated by papers dealing with complex technical and operational issues facing the political risk investment insurance industry. Hence, the pledge of shares problem between insurers and lenders, the issues surrounding preferred creditor status, the pricing of political risk insurance, and the need for an enhanced breach of contract coverage were discussed in considerable depth. The challenge of devising a way to securitize political risk investment insurance was also examined in great detail and commented on by senior representatives from Aon, Wharton, MIGA, ECGD (Export Credits Guarantee Department, United Kingdom), and EDC. (It was notable that no one argued that the securitization of political risk investment was likely the foreseeable future. *This certainly proved to be accurate.*)

Although general optimism about the future of the political risk investment insurance industry was implicit in many papers, the focus of the 2000 symposium was on addressing immediate obstacles or problems. The sole exception was an appendix paper by Gerald T. West and Keith Martin, titled "Political Risk Investment Insurance: The Renaissance Revisited" (West and Martin 2001).

Subsequent to a review of the macro factors affecting the political risk investment insurance market and the changes in the previous few years, West and Martin attempted *to net out* all the various driving factors to determine the magnitude and direction of the market. In this respect, they offered a number of observations (*Brief reflections on and critiques of their forecasts are offered in italics*):

1. Stimulated by losses to uninsured investors, and notwithstanding stagnation in investment flows, the issuance of investment insurance will rise. (*From a macro perspective, this forecast proved to be inaccurate; very little growth occurred in the succeeding period.*)
2. In the political risk investment insurance area, capacity will remain steady and premium rates should remain relatively stable. (*In the aftermath of the events of September 11, 2001, private capacity shrank and rates tended slightly upward. Subsequently, capacity slowly increased and rates softened.*)
3. There will be sharper differences in the treatment afforded uninsured investors, privately insured investors, and national or multilateral investors. The value of deterrence will be more clearly established. (*There is some evidence that this has occurred, but the value of deterrence is not yet firmly established.*)
4. Assembly of limited recourse debt financing for large infrastructure projects will be very difficult without long-term investment insurance. Cooperation and collaboration among insurers on these large projects should grow. (*There was a dramatic falloff in the number of limited-recourse, large infrastructure projects that were undertaken in the early 2000s for reasons having nothing to do with the availability of political risk investment insurance. With respect to the projects that did go forward, there was considerable evidence of greater cooperation among insurers.*)
5. After the recent dramatic increases in tenor in the private market (increasing from 1–3 years to 10–15 years), there will be no further extensions in the near future and there will be greater price variation for tenor. (*Subsequent to the events of September 11, 2001, there was an actual contraction in the availability of longer-term coverages, and a decline occurred in capacity; there was greater rate variation based on tenor.*)
6. As a result of significant losses in political risk investment insurance in 1999 and 2000, insurers and reinsurers will reexamine their rates, project limits,

and country limits. The result will be more variation across insurers a
nd hence a greater need for buyers to shop their insurance needs. (*This
re-examination did occur, and limits were altered. Considerable variations
among insurers did require investors and their brokers to shop and compare
insurers' offerings to best fill their needs.*)

The 2002 Symposium: The Brave New World

The events of September 11, 2001, and the full effect of the Argentine crisis
dramatically changed the atmosphere in which the third symposium was held
in October 2002. In a series of papers written from both demand- and supply-
side perspectives, as well as from public and private insurer perspectives, it was
clear that the euphoria of the late 1990s had completely disappeared. Insurance
providers, brokers, and investors were trying to look forward through a much
more opaque windshield.

The difficulties extended far beyond the events of September 11 and the
Argentine crisis (West 2004). There was a global economic slowdown, energy
prices were volatile, FDI fell by more than 25 percent, and nonbank private
lending fell by 70 percent. All these events directly affected the political risk
investment insurance market. Demand for ECGD and Lloyd's coverages in
that market fell in 2002 to about half of the demand in 2001 (Brown 2004).
Berne Union members' issuance of coverage fell from a peak of about US$17
billion in 2001 to less than US$12 billion in 2002. The ratio of investment
insurance coverage issued by Berne Union members to FDI flows hovered
around 6 percent.

The private political risk investment insurance industry entered a "hard"
phase. The hardening of the general insurance market was coupled with radical
reductions in reinsurance capacity. Tenors were severely affected (generally
down to five to seven years or less); capacity was restricted (30–50 percent
reductions for most private insurers); and pricing increased (up 10–20 percent).
The operating environment changed from a dynamic and flexible marketplace
to a harder and more cautious shadow of itself.

Yet at least one author pointed out that the resiliency of the political risk
investment insurance marketplace to temporary adversity should not be underestimated. There were three stout pillars on which the industry could rebuild.
First, there were at least three times the number of knowledgeable underwriters, lawyers, and brokers in 2002 than in 1992. Second, there were many more
"successful coverage models" to follow, modify, or build upon. Third, there was
an inherent flexibility stemming from having national, multilateral, and private
providers—many of whom were more willing than ever to work with one
another. Although they were competitors to some extent, political risk investment insurers were also becoming more aware of their shared interests and the
benefits of partnerships (West 2004).

The 2002 Symposium: The Supply Side

Five different perspectives on the events following September 11, 2001, and the Argentine crisis on the supply side were offered at the 2002 symposium by representatives of the public, private, and reinsurance communities.

Vivian Brown

Vivian Brown, then Chief Executive of ECGD and President of the Berne Union, started by observing that the twin crises had dented the confidence of investors in private political risk investment insurers and that there had been a move to "quality and safer" markets. He further argued that the way claims are settled in Argentina would influence investor perceptions of the value of political risk investment insurance.

Brown noted the rise in demand for "pure terrorism" coverage and the current stagnation in overall demand for political risk investment insurance coverages. He stated that once investment recovered and demand for such coverages increased, "public providers can expect to see more business while private insurers remain reluctant to take on more risk." He further stated: "As emerging markets open up to foreign investment and private capital flows, we can expect the shift away from export credits to continue while [political risk investment insurance] continues to rise." (Brown 2004, p. 19)

Reflections

Brown presciently noted the importance of the stability that the public providers of political risk investment insurance bring to the marketplace in times of volatility. He also identified the significant harm that could come to all insurers if the value of political risk investment coverage is seen by investors as illusionary. Finally, he accurately noted that all political risk investment insurance providers faced challenging times ahead.

However, Brown underestimated the resiliency of the private providers of political risk investment insurance in slowly rebuilding themselves in subsequent years—aided by the profitability of their terrorism coverages. Issuance of coverage by public sector political risk investment insurers did not rise, but tended to stagnate or decline; it certainly did not grow relative to their export credit business.

David James

David James, then Senior Underwriter for Ascot Underwriting Ltd., provided a London perspective on the effects of September 11, 2001, and the Argentine crisis. He noted that, although these events paralyzed large sections of the insurance community, the political risk investment insurance market responded well to the challenges. The insurance industry as a whole sustained a massive loss in the September 11 events and had to sell major stock positions in a declining and nervous market. The political risk investment insurers' need to rebuild their balance sheets will persist for some years.

Had it not been for the September 11 events, the Argentine crisis would have been the primary focus of political risk investment insurers. James noted that the crisis would be an important test of the presumptions of insurers and insureds and that it would retrospectively test the risk assessment methods of both sides and undoubtedly lead to modifications in their practices.

Subsequent to a review of the current supply-demand balance, James did not foresee rapid or dramatic changes in premium rates or market conditions, with policy periods generally capped in the three to five year range.

Reflections

James foresaw that the major losses occasioned by the Argentine crisis would truly test the value of the political risk investment insurance product. Although he—and most other observers—did not foresee the decade-long protracted "resolution" of the Argentine crisis, it did prove to be a watershed event for the industry. Many insureds were quite pleased that they had purchased coverage, but the silent minority who were able to get funds out of Argentina (or who obtained claims payments) were drowned out by the cries of the majority who suffered massive losses (or found that they did not have a valid claim against their insurers because of devaluation exclusions).

Stand-alone terrorism coverage proved to be a lucrative, but gradually declining, source of income for political risk investment insurers in subsequent years. Political risk insurers subsequently paid much more attention to the country spread of risk. Perhaps reflecting Ascot's diversified demand base for political risk investment insurance coverages, James did not venture any specific estimates of macro political risk investment insurance demand. There were no dramatic changes in premium rates or in policy tenors in the subsequent few years. Capacity, on both a per project and a per country basis, gradually improved for private insurers.

John Salinger

John Salinger noted that although the events of September 11, 2001, did not cause a single loss in the political risk insurance market, it nonetheless had seriously affected the entire industry. He noted, as others had done, the shrinkage in capacity and the shortening of policy tenors; however, he observed: "It may be surprising to regard these developments as a positive development, but the private insurance market has grown too large, and a correction was necessary."

Salinger noted that the events of September 11 had both a direct technical effect on insurance markets and an effect on the global risk environment. The immediate technical effect resulted in hardening rates and a dramatic reduction in reinsurance capacity—both of which hit the Lloyd's market particularly hard. A combination of factors, including the September 11 events; a global recession; the bursting of the dot-com bubble; the collapse of Enron, WorldCom, and Adelphia; the Argentine crisis; and other negative phenomena contributed to a general undermining of business confidence in the global environment. The perception of risk rose and has affected both investors and insurers.

Salinger asked: "What is the impact of all these factors on [political risk investment insurance]?" He forecasted that the private political risk investment insurance market will shrink further and that it will be very difficult to arrange coverage beyond a 10-year horizon. Although normally these events cause rates to rise, Salinger predicted that this rise will probably not happen because demand will remain soft. Public sector insurers will continue to increasingly collaborate with one another. With a smaller private sector, project sponsors will be forced to use public sector capacity.

Finally, Salinger observed that a few years ago markets refused to believe "bad news," and today they refuse to believe "good news." But he optimistically noted that "gloom and doom" will pass and there will be better days ahead.

Reflections

The era of gloom and doom obviously persisted for some time after these 2002 comments, and further bad news served to continue to depress the market. The recovery of the private political risk investment insurance market was a protracted process—especially with respect to the tenor of policies. The private market did shrink further, but the number of players did not change dramatically. Largely because of limited demand, rates remained soft for a considerable period. Although more collaboration occurred between political risk investment insurers, public insurers did not flourish—largely because they faced the same paucity of demand facing private insurers.

Brian Duperreault

Brian Duperreault, then chairman and Chief Executive Officer of Ace Limited, provided a reinsurer's perspective on the effects of the events of September 11, 2001, and the Argentine crisis. (Ace, and its affiliates, had become one of the world's largest providers of political risk investment insurance capacity.) He confirmed what other presenters had asserted concerning the effects of these events on the insurance industry in general, and on the political risk investment insurance industry in particular. The major losses associated with September 11 have had a significant effect on the capacity of the industry to accept risk. Although political risk investment insurance policy language had become more broad and general in the late 1990s, after September 11 insurers tightened their terms and conditions and tended to cover named perils only. Reinsurance markets had tightened, and political risk investment insurance was beginning to feel the results. Nearly all insurance premiums hardened in the aftermath of September 11. Terrorism, previously written on a stand-alone basis, was being written on a catastrophe basis; but coverage limits were a serious constraint.

Duperreault observed that Argentina will be viewed as a test case for the effectiveness of political risk investment insurance coverage; Ace had already paid several claims in Argentina, but the full effect of the crisis on insurers was still unfolding. Political risk investment insurance providers who rely heavily on reinsurance will face difficulties and, as a result, their capacity and tenors will be markedly reduced. The retrenchment will be occasioned in part by potential political risk investment insurance losses in Argentina and by higher rates available in other lines of insurance, which, in turn, reduce the amount of reinsurance available for political risk investment insurance. In the near term, the reduction in political risk investment insurance capacity and in tenors will meet a slowdown in demand as FDI flows to emerging markets stagnate or decline further.

Duperreault noted that because Sovereign is structured as a net underwriting joint venture, it will not be affected as seriously by the general retrenchment in the reinsurance sector as other political risk investment insurance providers. He voiced confidence in his firm's stability, reliability, and commitment to writing political risk investment insurance business in the future.

Reflections

As previously noted, the reinsurance market's support for political risk investment insurance coverages was significantly reduced. As a net insurer, Sovereign was, in fact, less affected by the retrenchment that subsequently occurred in the political risk investment insurance market. The recovery of the private political risk insurers was much slower than anticipated. Although capacity gradually returned, the temporary reduction was not as much of a constraint as were the large infrastructure projects of the 1990s, which were the major drivers of demand, diminished in the wake of the Asian crisis and Argentine issues.

Argentina was indeed a test of the effectiveness of political risk investment insurance coverage not only by banks, but also by equity investors. Were the losses that occurred the result of devaluation? Breach of contract? Regulatory risk? These were some of the issues debated with respect to political risk investment insurance claims in the infrastructure area. One insurer denied a claim, arguing that, among other things, the devaluation caused the underlying contract to be breached and the policy excluded losses caused by devaluation. To some, this was a surprising interpretation of the policy language.

At this time, many banks were buying very limited coverage that only involved the risk of inconvertibility. Although there was a limited period of inconvertibility, the real problem was that many borrowers did not have the funds to repay the loans because of the devaluation. Either banks did not understand what they were buying or their senior management was unaware of the limitations on the cover. In any case, the insurance policies did not respond as expected, which was somewhat of a death knell for political risk investment insurance for some lenders. In addition, U.S. bank regulators determined that political risk investment insurance was no longer sufficient to remove the risk from country exposure reporting and that such cover needed to be comprehensive. The "check the box" approach to obtaining limited political risk investment insurance cover was over.

Julie Martin

Subsequent to a discussion of the general insurance marketplace, including the softness of the mid-to-late 1990s and the hardening of the 2001/02 period, Julie Martin addressed the effect of the September 11, 2001, events and the Argentine crisis on the political risk investment insurance marketplace. She noted that, in general, insurers have become more cautious, capacity had shrunk, pricing in the private market had increased slightly (10–20 percent), and tenors had been reduced.

Many insurers were processing Argentine claims, which made it difficult to estimate the effects on the political risk investment insurance market. The market for power projects hardened considerably because of serious problems in many countries, including Argentina, China, India (Dabhol), Indonesia, and República Bolivariana de Venezuela. The market for stand-alone terrorism coverage was strong and was likely to remain so.

Martin noted that the 1996–2001 period witnessed unprecedented growth, choice, and innovation in the political risk investment insurance marketplace. There was a hardening of that market with more conservative underwriting and an increase in the number of potential claims. With the global economy in recession and more firms viewing political risk investment insurance as a discretionary form of insurance, there has been decreased demand, greater adverse selection against insurers, and a greater exposure to potentially catastrophic loss by both investors and insurers.

Perceptions of risk have changed, with investors being much more concerned about devaluation or depreciation risks and about regulatory risk than previously. Capital markets have grown and are looking for risk transfer mechanisms. The political risk investment insurance industry is under pressure to innovate and respond to these risks. Private-public cooperation has improved and needs to continue to do so.

Reflections

Martin noted that the political risk investment insurance industry was at a crossroads and that the crisis in Argentina and other claims was testing it. There is a need for the development of new products and for underwriters to learn from complex claims experiences. She cogently observed that the unsettling times should not necessarily be a deterrent to growth, but should serve both as a stimulus for innovation and as a reminder for prudence.

The 2002 Symposium: The Demand Side

Several papers addressed reactions of investors and lenders to the then recent upheavals in the global economy from demand-side perspectives. Kenneth Hansen, a partner with Chadbourne and Parke, focused on infrastructure issues; Anne Predieri (Bank of America) and Audrey Zuck (Willis) provided a lender's perspective; and Daniel Riordan, then Executive Vice President of Zurich Emerging Market Solutions, offered some commentary on their papers. Rather than treating each paper separately, a collective summary will be offered, followed by some collective reflections.

Hansen noted that the history of the political risk investment insurance industry—including OPIC, MIGA, and the private providers—is filled with dynamic innovation and adjustments to changed circumstances. He identified two areas that posed particularly daunting challenges. The first area is the mismatch between the inconvertibility coverage offered by insurers and the need of infrastructure investors for protection against devaluation. Hansen cited an innovative pilot product offered in 2001 by OPIC to AES for a power project in Brazil (Tietê) as the kind of step that will partially meet the needs of infrastructure investors. The second area is the need for enhanced expropriation coverage to mitigate the risk of the host government's breach of contract. Several public and private entities have partially addressed this need through coverage of the arbitration clause of an investment contract or nonhonoring of guarantee coverage. Partial risk guarantees by multilateral entities also address the investor's need to deal with the risk of sovereign breach of contract. However, given the then recent record of forced renegotiation of infrastructure investment agreements, Hansen suggested that investors and lenders in infrastructure projects will be much more cautious in the future than they had been in the euphoria of the late 1990s. In the future, Hansen concluded, there is a critical role that public agency insurers can potentially play in accepting the sovereign risks associated with infrastructure projects.

Predieri and Zuck brought a lender's perspective to their metaphorically titled paper "Political Risk Insurance as Penicillin." Traditional political risk investment insurance coverages were a useful means of treating many ailments in the early years of investment in emerging markets, but now, like penicillin, they are limited in their ability to combat some new afflictions that have recently emerged. In brief, political risk investment insurance needs to be supplemented, or at least modified, to deal with new disorders and maladies. Private insurers, free of many of the constraints binding public sector insurers, are capable of responding quickly and flexibly to new challenges. Public insurers have strong credit ratings and enjoy unique salvage advantages in many situations. Although Predieri and Zuck applauded the new specialized "antibiotics" that had been developed, including arbitral award default coverage, convertibility or transfer coverage for capital markets, and liquidity facilities like Teitê, they argued that more such coverages are needed. In this regard, they specifically mentioned lenders' current concerns about regulatory risks and devaluation.

Predieri and Zuck noted that the political risk investment insurance market had changed significantly in the previous year. With capacity shrinking and rates firming—especially for terrorism coverage—investors and lenders had to wrestle with difficult cost-benefit analyses with respect to the purchase of political risk investment insurance coverages.

The challenge going forward is to determine whether the covered perils constitute a sufficient portion of the emerging market risk to justify the premium cost as a percentage of the overall risk margin. Although not sounding a death knell for political risk insurance, they stressed the importance to the industry of the development of new products or the evolution of traditional products to meet investors' new needs.

Riordan noted that with the expected decline in international trade and investment in 2002 and 2003, there will be a reduction in overall demand for political risk investment insurance. This will, in particular, include international lenders, infrastructure investors, and capital market investors. Declining capacity and higher ceding commissions for reinsurance are expected to result in the hardening of prices, reduced tenors, and restricted coverages.

With respect to the future, Riordan stated his expectation that public agencies will continue to retract from the political risk investment insurance market as private insurers grow to fulfill the needs of investors and lenders. Public insurers will provide additional capacity for large projects and continue to serve segments of the market not well served by private insurers—small business and high-risk countries. The private market will continue to grow, albeit at a gradual pace and with dependency on available sources of reinsurance. Public agencies will serve their public policy roles as wholesalers of capacity or as reinsurers. The result will be an innovative and responsive marketplace.

Reflections

For a variety of reasons, and notwithstanding the innovativeness that Hansen argued has characterized the political risk investment insurance industry, satisfactory solutions to Hansen's two daunting challenges in the infrastructure area have yet to be discovered. The Tietê type of coverage has not been adopted on a widespread basis; nor has the devaluation conundrum been resolved. Coverage of capital market offerings has slowly expanded the participation of bondholders in emerging market projects. However, the heavy demand for political risk investment insurance coverage of infrastructure projects in the late 1990s has not been mirrored in the 2002–10 period. This situation is a partial reflection of the steep drop (50 percent from the peak in 1996) in the volume of new private power projects—a decline that persisted for many years. It also reflects the widespread political, economic, and operational problems besetting investors in the power sector in emerging markets. Finally, it is also the result of the caution (or as some might characterize it, the lack of boldness) demonstrated by public and private insurers alike as they struggled with many claims and disputes in the infrastructure area.

Notwithstanding history and the need for innovation that Predieri, Zuck, and Riordan discussed, there was an underestimation of the degree to which much lower demand sapped both the ability and the willingness of political risk investment insurers to devote resources to the development of new products in subsequent years. In the private market, capacity was very slow to return to the political risk investment insurance sector, in part because of the difficulty of securing reinsurance. Just as investors and lenders "hunkered down" in subsequent years, so too did many political risk investment insurers. This is not to say that innovative deals were not undertaken, but the intense demand (or stimuli) that nourished innovation in the late 1990s was clearly less evident in the 2002–10 period.

Although public insurers have stepped into reinsurance roles with greater frequency, they have not generally become wholesalers, nor have they faded away to fill only narrow market niches. They have continued to provide an element of stability in the political risk investment insurance market. The Berne Union has increasingly welcomed private insurers to its ranks, and collaboration among insurers has continued to increase.

The 2002 Symposium: Finding Common Ground or Uncommon Solutions

Given the challenges facing both the political risk investment insurance suppliers and the needs of those on the demand side, this section of the 2002 symposium asked where and how the twain shall meet. Felton "Mac" Johnston (FMJ International Risk), Edie Quintrell (then of OPIC), and David Bailey (Sovereign Risk) offered their observations. (As in the previous section, a collective summary will be offered, followed by some reflections.)

Johnston provided an optimistic perspective on the political risk investment insurance marketplace. In his view of the industry's history, investors, lenders, and insurers have always had to learn as they go, accumulating new experience—and sometimes developing new products—to help them cope with constantly surprising events. Even in the midst of retrenchment and uncertainty, there are grounds for optimism. Claims are bad news for both insurers and insureds, but they help everyone to better understand the risks and the policies that purport to address these risks and, hence, allow insurers to make improvements in the future.

Johnston iterated the "good news" for political risk investment insurance: There was more capacity in 2002 than 10 years before, even if capacity has temporarily declined; and political risk investment insurance has earned legitimacy and is accepted by major players. There is much more competition from both private and public sources, which is good for buyers. There is a growing body of experience—the number of investment insurance underwriters had roughly doubled between 1997 and 2002, and many of those underwriters had prior public sector experience—that facilitates cooperation and contributes to mutual understanding. Finally, Johnston noted that although demand—and the political risks driving it—may decline, it will not cease. Demand will experience a resurgence sooner or later. In sum, while Johnston acknowledged that the industry faces challenges, he believed that the foundations are sound and the prospects for the future are good.

Edie Quintrell, then Manager of the Insurance Department at OPIC, observed that broker and investor requests drive innovation and induce improvements in coverage—which then makes insurers more relevant and responsive to current conditions. For that result to take place, however, it is important that brokers and investors understand the institutions they are dealing with and the constraints under which they operate.

In the 2002 market, with private political risk investment tenors shortening and their capacity contracting, Quintrell suggested that it was difficult to expect innovation. She noted, "As long as Argentina remains unstable, as long as we experience the aftermath of September 11, the impact of the U.S. war on terrorism, and the effects of the war with Iraq," the political risk investment insurance market would continue to be hard. She foresaw insurers becoming both more conservative and more reluctant to take on new risks or to broaden their coverages. This situation obviously constituted an opportunity for public insurers to satisfy investor demand for coverage of risks that private insurers are unwilling or unable to underwrite.

David Bailey, formerly of EDC and currently with Sovereign, reviewed the history and evolution of the political risk investment insurance industry before commenting on the then present and likely future status of the industry. He noted that the 2002 operating environment presented a unique set of circumstances and challenges for the political risk investment insurance market. Client demands had intensified and become more focused on specific risks. Although both buyers and sellers had become more knowledgeable about the actual scope of coverage under political risk investment insurance policies, many were anxiously awaiting the specifics of how and why each Argentine project was resolved.

Bailey noted that the motivations of buyers had also undergone significant change—citing the institutional lenders' business as an example. In that particular case, the proposed Basel II regulatory changes may make the scope of political risk investment insurance policies a much more important factor in banks' purchase decisions. Many bank directors and shareholders are now actively interested in political risk investment insurance decisions.

Political risk investment insurance providers are now also operating under greater scrutiny from their shareholders and their reinsurers—most of whom experienced losses resulting from the events of September 11, the Enron collapse, and other catastrophes. Everyone was well aware of the many Argentine claims in the market.

Bailey asked: What will be the outcome of all of these recent events? The short answer is greater transparency. Insurers will be subject to greater disclosure. Banks and equity clients will need to be more open regarding the level of risk they accept. There is a considerable need for greater transparency with respect to claims information. The political risk investment insurance industry has traditionally not been open about releasing claims details. This approach, Bailey argued, is not in the best interest of the industry—especially when the political risk investment insurance product is under great scrutiny.

In sum, Bailey was confident in the future of political risk investment insurance. The product had undergone considerable enhancement and development in response to its clients in the past; Bailey expected that financially strong and creative providers would continue to meet the challenge.

Reflections

In the face of so many difficulties articulated by many different presenters, it was unusual to witness quiet confidence in the future by three veteran participants in the political risk investment insurance industry. The eight years following the 2002 symposium could be characterized in many ways—one could point to progress and innovation, but one could also point to a period of slow recovery that perhaps presages another period of growth and innovation. Argentine problems are still with us, concern about terrorism remains, and although the war in Iraq wanes, the war in Afghanistan remains. One adage seems to sum it up—"It was a period [2002–10] better than one feared, not as good as one hoped."

The Iraq war and the events of September 11 highlighted the need for cover against various forms of political violence. Because terrorism cover was typically included in standard property cover and then immediately excluded after September 11, new capital entered the market to fill the void. As with any new insurance product, terrorism cover was priced quite high initially—as much as 10 percent rate on line. Over time, as fewer events and losses have occurred, the rate has come down dramatically. Another issue that emerged was whether terrorism was the right cover for companies with exposure in emerging markets because it excluded war, civil war, insurrection, and other forms of political violence. There was a brief period when full political violence cover could be placed at less cost than a terrorism policy because there underwriting approaches varied and because the covers were handled by different groups within a single insurer. Over time, this anomaly has disappeared, but questions remain about where terrorism coverage ends and other political violence perils begin.

The 2004 Symposium: Perspectives of the Future

Three articles written for the November 2004 symposium are of particular note because they addressed the possible future evolution of the industry: Clive Tobin, then CEO of XL Insurance, wrote "The Future of the International Political Risk Insurance Industry"; Toby Heppel, then of FirstCity Partnership Ltd added "Perspectives on Private-Public Relationships in Political Risk Insurance"; and Gerald T. West and Kristofer Hamel, both of MIGA, contributed "Whither the Political Insurance Industry?" Collectively, these three articles presented a broad characterization of the potential evolution of the political risk investment insurance industry. This section examines these articles from the perspective of six years later.

Clive Tobin

Clive Tobin prefaced his analysis of the political risk investment insurance industry with a review of the global insurance industry in the recent past. Noting in particular the effect of the insurance cycle, he briefly explored the links between the mainstream insurance markets (and their low profitability in the previous five years), the reinsurance market, and the effects on the private political risk investment insurance market.

The momentous events of September 11, 2001, and the catastrophic losses that resulted (although not political risk investment losses), pulled capital into the property and casualty market to take advantage of the inevitable upcycle benefits that would follow. The result was a significant contraction in private sector political risk investment capacity. From a peak in 2000 when at least US$1 billion in private capacity for a single risk could be theoretically assembled, by 2002 that sum was well under US$1 billion. More significant, risk tenors were severely cut back. Tobin estimated that, in comparison with 2001, by 2004 less than half of the 10-year exposure capacity in the private political risk investment insurance market was available.

Other dynamics affected the political risk investment industry as well, including stagnation in cross-border lending and investment and the fact that existing investors cut back their political risk investment insurance budgets to pay for material price increases on other insurance coverages. Ironically, political risk investment insurance pricing in the private market was on a downward track between 2002 and 2004, in part because slim bank margins had driven prices downward.

Regarding the relationships between public and private insurers, Tobin found himself in broad agreement with Toby Heppel's positive comments (see below) about the benefits to both sectors as a result of their collaboration. This result was illustrated by the way both sectors faced the common challenges of the Argentine and Venezuelan crises.

Tobin noted that developments in the reinsurance markets have had a direct effect on the private political risk investment insurance industry. Reinsurers began to restrict the amount of political risk investment insurance coverage they were willing to provide in 2001, and the September 11 and Argentine crises occurring later that year exacerbated the trend. Hence, for the 2002–05 period, there would be capacity restrictions, a pullback on policy tenors, and restrictions on coverage. Reinsurers were also struggling with a concentration of exposure problem. Among some 30 significant private political risk investment insurers, there was a significant degree of correlation and concentration of political risk investment risks written. Thus, there was limited opportunity for reinsurers to differentiate those risks—and therefore to satisfy the demands of all the direct players.

Turning to the future, Tobin asserted that a softening market will generally be a good thing for political risk insurers because it will attract greater capital; hence, the tight grip reinsurers have on the political risk investment insurance market will be loosened. Tobin expected some easing of the tenors and conditions imposed by reinsurers by 2005. With fewer reinsurers, however, there may be a reinsurance focus on providing coverage to only the best direct underwriters.

Dusting off his crystal ball, Tobin was of the view that capacity among private insurers will come back, FDI and international lending will increase, political risk investment insurance demand will increase, and overall risk factors in emerging markets will look better. Given these trends, Tobin noted three areas of concern:

1. The concentration of coverages in the "Big Five" countries has caused capacity problems that the industry needs to address. The need to improve the spread of risk across countries has become more important.
2. The need to plan for more coverage of infrastructure projects is clear. Private insurers need to overcome their wariness about this sector while avoiding the pitfalls of the past.
3. Private insurers need to look at demand in a wider range of countries. Working with public insurers may be a prerequisite to doing so.

Private, specialist insurers have carved out a permanent niche for themselves in providing coverage through the insurance cycle. That said, Tobin acknowledged that in the past insurers and insureds have had differences of opinion over what was covered and not covered. It is vital, he asserted, that insureds know what they are buying and that insurers are clear as to what is covered and what is not covered. Although investment risks can be complex, the uncertainty in insurance products must be reduced before deals are done. Given that contractual exposure to investment risks is unlikely to fall, insurers need to appraise and price these exposures appropriately. Tobin noted that the political risk market went through turbulent times in the 2001–04 period and survived in reasonably good shape. He concluded by noting XL's commitment to public-private partnerships and his cautious optimism about the future.

Reflections

XL Insurance subsequently exited the political risk investment insurance market, both as a direct underwriter through their Lloyd's syndicate in 2007 and as a partner with ACE in Sovereign. The ostensible reason was a change of strategy in what they wanted to offer and how they wanted to provide it.

Tobin was accurate in his projection that capacity would return (despite XL's withdrawal). It is interesting that despite substantial credit claims paid over the past two years by many insurers, political risk investment insurance capacity has remained relatively stable. Insurers seem to have become more conservative about what to cover and are less likely to use their full limits or maximum tenors.

Tobin's predictions that FDI, international lending, and demand for political risk investment insurance would increase were correct in the short term, but they declined in the medium term. Although one could argue that the emerging market countries have weathered the global financial crisis better than most developing countries, it is not clear that the overall risk factors in emerging markets have improved on an aggregate basis.

Toby Heppel

Toby Heppel began his paper with an assessment of the differences in role, motivation, and operational approach between the public and private sector political risk insurers. Given the different purposes for which these insurers exist (public policy versus profit), the private insurers are notably free of the restrictive eligibility criteria that bind most public insurers. This situation, in turn, influences their operational practices and their pricing strategy. Public insurers tend to price according to their appraisal of market risk; private insurers charge on the basis of market conditions.

Heppel examined the convergence, competition, and cooperation "revolutions" that emerged in the 1990s between the private and public sectors. Initially, the tenor of the private insurers was too short (three years) to compete with public insurers. In 1995–96, Lloyd's syndicates and AIG began offering seven-year coverage, and, subsequently, AIG began offering 10- and 15-year coverage under some circumstances. However, initial friction between the two sectors increasingly gave way to collaboration, partnerships, and the search for solutions to common problems. Both sides began recognizing the benefits of partnership arrangements. The private insurers gained access to business that they might otherwise not encounter, to mitigation that might reduce the likelihood of loss or increase the likelihood of recovery (the so-called halo effect), and to specialized information. The key role of the public sector insurers in the leadership and mobilization of insurance capacity for large, complex risks was recognized. The public sector, in turn, benefited from novel ideas for coverage and contract language, techniques for administering and servicing portfolios, risk transfer, and capacity enhancement.

There were and are many practical difficulties that needed to be addressed in these public-private arrangements—especially relating to claims processing and management. But with each successful collaboration, the next coinsurance or reinsurance arrangement became somewhat easier. Overall, argued Heppel, both sectors learned that the actual experience of working cooperatively yielded benefits that far outweighed their difficulties.

This collaborative process has been abetted by three factors: the growing maturity of many private insurers as they better understand their public sector counterparts; the transfer of experience and expertise by senior figures in the public sector as they migrate to private insurer positions; and private sector membership in the Berne Union.

Heppel acknowledged that although public-private cooperation "is here to stay," how this cooperation may evolve depends on many factors beyond the control of any insurer. Trends and market conditions might continue as they existed in 2004. Alternatively, there might be simultaneous crises of grand proportion that force major contractions in private sector capacity. New techniques for managing portfolios of risks or expanding capacity, such as credit default swaps and securitization, might fundamentally alter the parameters for public-private cooperation. The health of the global reinsurance marketplace will heavily influence the tenors and capacity that private investment insurers can offer. Substantial losses in close proximity to other sectors (for example, hurricanes, floods, earthquakes) will harden the reinsurance market and severely affect political risk investment insurance capacity.

Finally, as did Clive Tobin, Heppel acknowledged that there is demand for currency devaluation coverage, but that it is unlikely, in his view, to be addressed by the industry.

Reflections

Heppel discussed and projected the growth of public-private cooperation and the cross-fertilization of the two parts of the industry. Although the cooperation continued to improve after 2004, it seems to have stabilized and leveled off. The organizations' different objectives and their focus on slightly different segments of the market mean that the opportunities for cooperation on coverages will always face some limits. Certainly, a transfer of ideas through the Berne Union and its working groups has continued.

Heppel's list of factors that might affect the development of the two markets has been accurate, but in a muted way. Hurricane Katrina, credit default swap crises, and other similar phenomena have affected the political risk investment insurance market, but not dramatically and only at the edges.

Gerald T. West and Kristopher Hamel

West and Hamel (W&H) began their article, titled "Whither the Political Risk Insurance Industry," by noting that many factors on both the supply side and the demand side will shape the course of the industry. Initially exploring the hypothesis that the industry's future will be primarily shaped by international investment flows or by the general economic environment, W&H found that argument flawed and instead found that the future is more likely to be shaped by many other factors.

Although acknowledging the common belief that the "tidal flow" of new FDI, whether rising or falling, carries the volume of issuance of political risk investment insurance coverage upward or downward, W&H found that this was not the case in the 1990–2000 period. Their empirical analysis revealed that although the aggregate coverage issued by Berne Union members *steadily increased* from 1990 to 2000, the percentage of FDI flows to emerging markets that was covered by political risk investment insurance *steadily decreased* from about 11 percent to 4 percent. During a period of declining FDI flows from 2000 to 2003, aggregate coverage issued by Berne Union members tended to increase, rising to about 9 percent in 2003. Issuance of investment insurance coverage by any one insurer (such as MIGA) showed considerable variation from both aggregate Berne Union statistics and FDI flows. W&H concluded that there were obviously more complex factors at work on both the supply and the demand sides that were shaping the evolution of the political risk investment insurance industry.

On the supply side, the presence of public insurers appears to be an element of stability for the political risk investment insurance market. However, the veneer of stability is frequently altered by policy changes (especially related to their individual eligibility criteria) that affect their underwriting decisions. As was previously noted by Tobin and Heppel, the private sector is significantly affected on the supply side by the general health of the insurance industry and the current position of the market in the insurance and reinsurance cycles. Private sector insurers are able to offer freedom from national eligibility and policy restrictions, flexible coverage, and swift issuance of policies. Fueled by competition and new entrants such as Sovereign and Zurich in 1997, the growth of private political risk investment insurance coverage has burgeoned. Frictions between private and public insurers arose, but the natural differences in their core markets have encouraged greater cooperation and collaboration.

W&H noted that on the supply side, there is considerable elasticity. Many national and multilateral entities have the capacity to write much higher levels of coverage, and private insurers can expand their issuance of coverage very swiftly. Hence, on the supply side, there are few hard limits on the ability of investment insurers to issue substantially more coverage than they have in the past.

On the demand side for political risk investment insurance, W&H note that the situation is much more complex. The users of such insurance are heterogeneous and seek (or decline to seek) coverage for many different reasons. Certainly there are some defensive buyers who respond to broad country, regional, or global trends—the activities of a Fidel Castro or a Hugo Chavez clearly stimulated demand for political risk investment coverages in Latin America. Projects with limited recourse project finance necessarily focused attention on the pricing and allocation of political risk—often to the benefit of political risk investment insurers. Conversely, the decline of such deals evaporated demand from that quarter. Natural resource investors who must venture into exotic locales where instability is the norm are natural users of political risk investment insurance. However, the heterogeneity of investors and their risk management proclivities make it very difficult to estimate the future demand for political risk investment coverages.

Moreover, there is much more information about operating conditions in emerging markets than ever before. This has served to make investors more comfortable and less uncertain about the protection of their assets and property rights. Improved laws and regulations in many emerging markets have also contributed to reducing investor anxiety. W&H noted that banks, facing the need to satisfy their Basel II requirements concerning capital allocation, should be a significant source of future demand for political risk investment insurance.

W&H concluded that given the numerous macro and micro factors that will influence the future evolution of the political risk investment insurance market, it is exceptionally difficult to consider the interactions of these factors and to "net them out" to understand the possible magnitude and future direction of the market. The possible decline, stagnation, or growth of the political risk investment insurance industry is treated in very broad terms. From the perspective of early 2005, W&H argued that for multiple reasons, decline is unlikely. However, in discerning the possible paths between stagnation and growth, they asserted that the prognosis is more difficult.

In addition to exogenous factors that could affect this small, fragile line of coverages, a considerable number of internal forces could contribute to stagnation in the political risk investment insurance industry. These forces include underinvestment in new product development, the potential departure of key staff underwriters and the lack of adequate training of new underwriters, periodic upheavals in the leadership and policies of public political risk investment insurers, and new competition from entities offering broad financial guarantees. All these forces could contribute to ossification in the industry; at a minimum, they political risk investment insurers will have difficulty building a balanced portfolio of risks.

W&H acknowledged that certain factors could contribute to growth in the political risk investment insurance industry. The forces of globalization both push and pull Organisation for Economic Co-operation and Development investors toward emerging markets. Many firms are first-time investors in emerging markets and are thus predisposed to consider investment insurance—especially in the growing group of investors from those markets venturing into other emerging countries (the so-called South-South investors). Prices for many mineral and energy commodities are high, which will make these commodities (with their high initial capital investments) prime candidates for political risk investment coverages. Pervasive problems associated with infrastructure projects in the energy and water sectors will also make new investments in those sectors attractive candidates for coverage.

W&H noted that the future health of the PRI industry is not a deterministic result of macro forces (numerous as they may be). Political risk insurance is a product, they asserted, that does not sell itself. It must be sold by knowledgeable brokers and underwriters who demonstrate the flexibility of this instrument to meet the particular needs of each equity or debt investor. The need for industry members to both educate new investors and actively market their products is high—and will likely determine the overall robustness of the industry in the future.

Reflections

W&H made a compelling case that FDI flows are not the primary predictor of demand for political risk investment insurance. However, their efforts to identify, sort through, and "net out" the effects of different factors were only partially successful. Although W&H argued that a decline for political risk investment insurance is unlikely, many underwriters and brokers would argue from the perspective of 2010 that their political risk investment insurance books are declining, while their credit books are increasing because of Basel II–based demand (which has been a stimulus, as correctly predicted by W&H and others). Even where an insurer's political risk investment insurance book of business is not declining, this situation often occurs because of the demand for nonhonoring coverage by banks—the political parallel to credit cover where the borrower is a government entity.

According to W&H, any future stagnation in the political risk investment insurance industry might be partially the result of inadequate marketing of underwriters' services. Many in that business would dispute that argument. Many public underwriters spend substantial resources on promoting their programs. Informative websites of both private and public insurers are the norm. In addition, the number of informative websites by brokers has increased substantially.

The number of dedicated political risk brokers has ebbed and flowed somewhat not only in relation to their individual company's successes, but also with the market. However, the percentage of business that is brokered versus the percentage that is direct has increased for virtually all private insurers. This fact is at least a partial indicator of successful marketing of political risk investment insurance coverages.

The 2006 Symposium: Forecasts for the Political Risk Investment Insurance Industry in 2010

Papers were written in mid-2006 for the fourth MIGA-Georgetown symposium held in November 2006 on the possible state of the political risk investment insurance industry in 2010. Five individuals were asked to peer though the "muddy windshield" of the future and describe the status of the political risk investment insurance industry in 2010.

John Salinger

John Salinger, a veteran of more than 30 years in this field, prefaced his three predictions about the future with a succinct review of his old predictions that have come to pass. With respect to the latter, he observed that the private sector had firmly established itself in the market and had moved to a position of rough equality with the national and multinational agencies in the area of investment insurance. Private insurers, he noted, have made themselves more compatible with national insurers like OPIC; this compatibility included, importantly, the extension of the tenor of policies first to seven years and then to 15 years. Coinsurance became more common between insurers. Seven private insurance underwriters were serving the U.S. market in 2006, and they had "never been more innovative or cooperative."

With respect to the political risk investment insurance industry in 2010, Salinger (2008, 201) hazarded three predictions:

1. "Collaboration between government and private underwriters will continue to deepen and will be manifest in the rising influence of the Berne Union."
2. "The insurance industry will not solve the problem of devaluation risk. The solution, if there is one, will come from commercial banks or the capital markets."
3. "Insurers will take steps to partially solve the problem of regulatory risk in emerging markets and the solution will be based on bilateral investment treaties."

Reflections

Regarding the first Salinger prediction, the Berne Union has grown to include many more insurers and has facilitated the sharing of expertise among members and in dealing with common problems. The Berne Union not only has expanded to 50 members (not counting an additional 25 members of the Prague Club), but also, starting with AIG in 1999, now includes 16 private sector entities. Both within and outside of the Berne Union, little doubt exists that there has been more collaboration among investment insurers regarding both coinsurance and reinsurance.

With respect to the second Salinger prediction, there is also little doubt regarding the fact that the political risk investment insurance industry has not solved the problem of devaluation. Moreover, a solution has not come forth from commercial banks or from the capital markets, nor does a solution—most observers would hazard—appear to be on the horizon.

With respect to the third Salinger prediction, there has admittedly been some progress "in partially solving the problem of regulatory risk," but whether progress to date can be attributed to bilateral investment treaties is arguable. Salinger suggested that a change in the basic contract language might provide coverage against unfair and inequitable treatment *as determined by an arbitration panel*. Certainly coverage of nonpayment of arbitral awards is much more commonly available in 2010 than it was in 2006. Salinger acknowledged then that the shortcoming of this approach was the time to get an award: "Some of the Argentine cases will take three to five years to reach a conclusion" (Salinger 2008, 201).

In sum, John Salinger's cautious predictions can be said to have been both modest in scope and reasonably accurate.

Christina Westholm-Schröder

Christina Westholm-Schröder, a veteran of more than 20 years in the political risk investment insurance industry, began by noting that many factors have affected and will continue to affect that industry. Many of these factors are known (including developments in the general insurance market and the reinsurance market), but many others—like the crisis in Argentina and the events of September 11, 2001—were neither known nor foreseen. Hence, she noted that predicting the future for the political risk investment insurance industry is not at all a straightforward task.

Westholm-Schröder identified one of the major challenges and opportunities facing the political risk investment insurance industry as the implementation of the Basel II framework. She asserted that, to remain relevant, "[political risk investment] insurers will start to offer unconditional guarantees" (as defined in the Basel II framework). "By 2010, we will all be doing that." She further argued that the regulatory requirements of Basel II will have a significant impact on the industry for the next few years.

Regarding the cost of coverage, Westholm-Schröder acknowledged that buyers of coverage would like to hear that in the future the cost of coverage will decrease. However, she noted that this situation is unlikely to occur across the board—and will not occur in markets where capacity is scarce. Political risk investment insurance pricing is based on many factors, but the two most fundamental factors are risk and available capacity.

Westholm-Schröder (2008, 211) stated: "The issue with the [political risk investment insurance] [in 2006]—which is not likely to change by 2010, or even by 2020—is that insurers are often close to their country limits in those markets where the demand is the greatest." Pricing in high-demand countries is capacity driven rather than risk driven. Political risk investment insurance "at 'bargain rates' is available in markets such as Croatia because insurers want to add risk there, but not in Russia, where insurers already have a lot of exposure" (Westholm-Schröder 2008, 211).

Reinsurers of political risk investment insurance providers also follow their own dynamics and tend not to want to provide more capacity should a country be deemed more risky. Hence, even as demand for coverage in a certain country might increase, provided capacity may decrease, thus further exacerbating the supply-demand imbalance.

Westholm-Schröder identified a score of factors that will influence supply and demand for political risk investment insurance products, but concluded that the product mix will remain similar in the future to that of 2006. High commodity prices will encourage new investments in extractive industries, and interest in "traditional" products (expropriation, war and political violence, currency inconvertibility, and nontransfer) will subsequently increase. There will be further development and refinement of banks' use of political risk investment insurance for regulatory capital.

With respect to devaluation coverage, Westholm-Schröder (2008, 213) noted that it is "not very likely that insurers will be offering this coverage, at least not on a significant scale." Coverage of local currency obligations is more likely.

With respect to cooperative relations among private and public insurers, Westholm-Schröder foresaw more public insurers buying reinsurance coverage from private providers. Both parties will recognize the benefits from portfolio diversification and there may even be some reinsurance of private market insurers.

Westholm-Schröder's succinct conclusion is worthy of noting in its entirety:

"To summarize, there are a multitude of factors that impact on the [political risk insurance] industry and our crystal ball is not flawless. Past prognostications are consistent in only one aspect: very few are exactly correct. Therefore, in order to succeed in the long run, an insurer will need to spend less time guessing what might happen and instead creating an organization that is flexible and creative enough to respond when the unexpected does happen. The [political risk insurance] industry needs to be there for the long run and have the ability and willingness to not only pay claims in a timely fashion, but also to meet clients' evolving demands for products and support that satisfy internal and external requirements of risk protection." (2008, 214)

Reflections

One common prediction running through both the 2006 symposium and previous symposia relates to the effect of Basel II on demand for cover by banks. Westholm-Schröder and others correctly predicted the adaptation of policies by insurers to allow banks to obtain some capital relief through the use of these policies. The policies are not "unconditional" as predicted, but are very streamlined such that the conditions are within control of the bank. Substantial work has been put into developing policies that are considered "Basel II compliant," but these policies vary by bank, by country, and by underwriter—although there are some common themes. Most of the demand has been for private sector risk and, interestingly, Sovereign does not offer that cover.

Westholm-Schröder foresaw that pricing was unlikely to decrease across the board and was fairly accurate in this regard. Despite some increased perceptions of risk, the market remained sufficiently liquid so that regardless of an increase in rates in the wake of the recent global financial crisis, premium rates have continued to be under pressure.

As Westholm-Schröder predicted, the product mix has remained similar, but this has been the case for decades. The basic perils are defined, and they can be applied to different forms of investment or trade. As with Salinger and others, Westholm-Schröder predicted that devaluation cover was unlikely to be offered—although Sovereign was the only insurer that appeared to have publicly adopted the Tietê model to provide liquidity to banks in the event of a devaluation.

High commodity prices did subsequently create some demand for coverage of extractive industry projects and certainly helped trigger expropriations or renegotiations of contracts in various countries—especially in South America. But this demand was relatively short-lived as some commodity prices dropped in the wake of the global financial crisis.

Finally, Westholm-Schröder estimated that there will be more public-private cooperation among insurers and, in particular, more private reinsurance of public providers. It is unclear whether what has occurred has been anything more than ad hoc agreements, but demand may increase in the future if and when public entities need more "head room."

Joanne Palmer

From the perspective of a public sector insurer, Joanne Palmer examined supply and demand trends in the political risk investment insurance industry in 2006 and then looked at products currently used by investors and international banks. She then offered her own medium-term predictions before closing with some observations about the future role of public sector insurers.

Looking back over 2001–05, Palmer noted that the major events (for example, the events of September 11, the crisis in Argentina, various hurricanes, and natural disasters) had only temporary negative effects on the growth of capacity in the international political risk investment insurance industry. There was a significant and general softening of the insurance market. Political risk investment insurance capacity rebounded with the entrance of new players, increases in project limits, and the strengthening of the reinsurance market. The competitive situation shrank premium rates to near-historic lows. Palmer observed that, barring widespread claims payments by political risk insurers (or a significant decrease in reinsurance capacity), there is no reason to foresee any reversal of this trend.

On the demand side, Palmer noted that FDI flows to Asia (especially China) were likely to remain strong, flows to Africa were strengthening, and flows to Latin America were (and would continue to be) mixed. In all regions, she noted that a good part of the investment had been in natural resources, with some strength in the power and communications sectors. Thus, although there seemed to be sufficient investment flows to places with political risk (and hence a potential role for political risk insurers), she asked, "Are investors and their lenders continuing to seek [political risk investment insurance]?"

Notwithstanding some negative events in 2006 (including overt actions by the governments of Bolivia, Ecuador, and Venezuela against natural resource investors, nuclear testing by the Democratic People's Republic of Korea, and bombings in the Middle East) that should serve to stimulate demand for insurance against expropriation and political violence, Palmer did not foresee a dramatic resurgence of demand for political risk investment insurance.

Palmer noted a contrary influence that emerged regarding the experience of investors and lenders in Argentina, where many political risk investment insurance policyholders discovered what was (and was not) covered by their policies. She also noted another demand factor—the emerging importance of Asian investors who are content to self-insure.

Palmer's conclusion with respect to demand is thus mixed—demand has been strengthened by reminders of events that are perils covered by traditional coverage, but there are residual concerns about the relevance of the product (and, by implication, its price) that are affecting the market.

Palmer then turned to some investor and lender viewpoints about the market that will shape its future evolution. Although investors are continuing to buy political risk investment insurance against the traditional perils of expropriation, political violence, and transfer and inconvertibility, they are demanding broader coverage from insurers. As a consequence of examining their political risk investment insurance coverage more closely, investors are pressing insurers to stretch their traditional coverage language to better cover investors' perceived needs. Thus, political violence coverage might be broadened to cover the threat of violence versus the actual loss or to cover temporary loss of income rather than asset damage. With respect to expropriation coverage, Palmer noted that there is pressure to more explicitly cover regulatory risk. Her expectation is that the political risk investment insurance industry will be flexible in its response to such demands—in part because it wishes to remain relevant to its clients' risk transfer needs and in part because these demands can be accommodated by tweaking existing coverage parameters rather than by shouldering the burdens of developing totally new products.

Palmer noted that the recent expansion of political risk investment insurance coverage to insure against the failure of a sovereign or quasi-sovereign to honor an arbitral award (that is, arbitral award default coverage) shows great promise if some details can be worked out. Selective investors will continue to be interested in the protection of multicountry portfolios of investments or assets (that is, a global policy). Although demand for such coverage will likely continue, the pricing of such coverage will remain a problem for both parties.

As did John Salinger, Palmer acknowledged that although investor demand for devaluation coverage will continue, it is very unlikely to be addressed by political risk investment insurers.

The protection of intellectual property rights is also an area of concern for investors. Palmer (2008, 219) noted that some discussion has taken place within some insurers on the subject and that "it is quite possible a product will emerge in the medium term."

Another unmet investor demand relates to bribery and corruption. Insurers are aware of this interest in a product that adequately protects an investor. Most public insurers have specific exclusions denying liability for such risks rather than covering them. Some investors, however, want protection against being forced to pay bribes to government officials in cases where such actions seem to be officially sanctioned by the government. Palmer (2008, 219) noted, "It is very doubtful that the insurance market will touch this risk any time soon."

Turning to lenders' concerns, Palmer noted that the high level of competition and low interest rate spreads mean that there is little room in the banks' pricing for political risk investment insurance premiums even if such coverage is desired. Moreover, the Argentine situation has induced many banks to look very carefully at their insurance contracts. There is particular concern over the waiting periods before a claim can be made. The result is greater selectivity by some banks as to when and where they seek coverage. Hence, difficult markets like those of Venezuela and the Democratic Republic of the Congo or complex financing structures with long tenures still attract interest in securing political risk investment insurance coverages.

Banks, of course, remain interested in comprehensive coverage (sometimes referred to as sovereign nonpayment coverage). Palmer noted that this coverage has become an important product for many insurers and expects that it will remain so. Banks can be expected to continue their efforts to stretch the parameters of this coverage with respect to the length of tenor, the type of loan structure, and, more important, the definition of "sovereign." From a Basel II provisioning perspective, banks will continue to push insurers to narrow the conditionality of their insurance policies so that the insurance is as close as possible to a guarantee.

Palmer expects that local currency financing and mezzanine financing will continue to grow and that these trends will generate some modest opportunities for insurers.

With the surge in private sector insurance capacity and the desire of public insurers to not displace private insurers, public sector providers face an extra challenge in both maintaining a healthy portfolio of risks and finding meaningful roles for themselves in the industry. Palmer noted that public sector insurers provide stability in the market, both in terms of providing capacity in difficult markets on a more sustained basis (because of high country limits) and in terms of pricing (if private capacity does become limited). Reinsurance arrangements between public and private insurers have benefited both parties. Coinsurance arrangements have allowed public sector insurers to leverage capacity from the private market for investments that a private insurer may be unwilling to venture alone because of risk considerations.

Palmer noted that some clients will continue to prefer a public sector insurer for various reasons. Many public insurers have a mandate to serve smaller investors that might otherwise be overlooked because of their size. Although public insurers are often viewed as cumbersome in terms of their processing times (especially because of their concern with environmental and social issues), in some circumstances this processing delay can be an attractive feature to investors because of the insurers' rigorous analysis of these issues.

Palmer noted that relations between public and private insurers will continue to evolve. Public insurers might well be the innovators in responding to investor needs and pushing the boundaries of traditional political risk investment insurance coverage.

In sum, Palmer noted that there is little to indicate any revolutionary changes to the political risk investment insurance market in the medium term. Insurers will continue to track trends in demands and will modify their coverages to accommodate developments in financing structures.

Reflections

Palmer's prediction on pricing was generally accurate in that she argued that prices would remain low barring widespread claims. The credit claims of 2008 and 2009, along with perception of increased risk, did put pressure on pricing for all lines of cover offered by political risk insurers. Despite the actions of Hugo Chavez and others, there has been no dramatic resurgence in demand for political risk investment insurance and, in fact, the financial crisis has had a dampening effect on the demand for coverage by banks and equity investors as well.

Palmer suggested that pricing of multicountry portfolios would remain a problem. In fact, it seems that multicountry political risk investment insurance portfolios were handled straightforwardly in the private sector until quite recently, as insurers have begun to reconsider the effect on their aggregate exposures. Palmer foresaw that there would be modest opportunities for coverage of local currency financings. This prediction appears to have been accurate, although many insurers are still struggling with the technical difficulties of providing such coverage. Intellectual property has not yet emerged as a product, although there is renewed discussion about it. With the growth in the private market and the stagnation in overall demand, some public sector providers have struggled to maintain a healthy and balanced portfolio; however, this situation appears to be the case for some, but not all, public insurers.

D. Greg Ansermino

Greg Ansermino, a director with Standard Bank of South Africa, provided some analyses from the perspective of a user of political risk investment insurance. With respect to supply-side drivers, he noted several trends. First, he observed that public sector insurers are becoming more sophisticated and working better in coinsurance and reinsurance relationships with their private sector counterparts. However, there are signs of "crowding out" of private insurers as some public insurers are becoming less focused on being "insurers of last resort." Public insurers are increasingly citing their deterrent capabilities. Elaborating on this situation, Ansermino noted that insurance consumers are becoming more sophisticated regarding their political risk investment insurance requirements; he made the distinction between a "hard" cover and a "soft" cover. In the former case, the insurer underwrites on the basis of expecting minimal recoveries. In the latter case, the insurer may have a multitude of other relationships with the host government through the insurer's shareholders or related entities, which can potentially influence both the host government's initial actions and its subsequent actions—including recoveries. Thus, the "soft" insurer becomes an active participant in risk mitigation. Ansermino argued that more astute project sponsors are beginning to understand this value; the future debate will be over the value of this "hard" versus "soft" difference.

Two other developments are cited on the supply side. First, some development finance institutions are now offering guarantee products that function as political risk mitigation tools. Second, some developing countries are creating and expanding their own export credit and investment insurance capabilities—often at submarket pricing. In both cases, it remains to be seen whether these two developments will affect the traditional political risk investment insurance market.

In sum, on the supply side Ansermino foresaw that political risk investment insurance capacity will increase and that pressure on pricing will occur in the medium term. The private market has already responded and is aggressively pricing in some preferred emerging market countries. With the public sector becoming more efficient and the private sector becoming more aggressive, the competition should benefit the consumer.

Ansermino next considered several fundamental macroeconomic factors that will shape the demand side for political risk investment insurance. Noting the burgeoning growth of the Chinese economy and the nascent growth of the Indian economy, Ansermino reflected on the implications for commodity markets. The amounts of iron ore, copper, cement, bauxite, and oil needed to fuel this growth will require massive new investments in many countries not known for political stability. Subsequently, the magnitude of the demand for political risk mitigation will be a challenge for traditional markets for political risk investment insurance. Adding to the complexity of this demand will be the complexity of sponsors and off-takers from emerging market countries that are barely investment-grade themselves. Weaknesses in the U.S. economy, globalization, and the energy crisis will all contribute additional complexity to the political risk situation for investors. Ansermino noted that in 2005, a few resource-risk developing countries (such as Bolivia and Venezuela) were already yielding to the temptation to flex their new-found bargaining strength. The challenge of mitigating political risk in the unstable Middle East will be of great importance to secure access to oil.

With respect to regulatory drivers, Ansermino asserted that the implications of Basel II will have profound consequences for the use of political risk investment insurance by the banking sector. The introduction of the Basel II requirements has reopened the debate around the value of such insurance; these requirements will have a fundamental effect on pricing and on the way that insurers and bankers interact. Although this process was still in its infancy, it was clear to Ansermino that banks will be spending much more time assessing risk and evaluating the cost to them of self-insurance versus political risk investment insurance.

Ansermino noted that high levels of corporate liquidity have made project finance less attractive; banks have been forced to look for new uses of their own capital. This has spurred innovation in structuring deals—including the management of political risk. Revenue streams denominated in local currencies pose particular risk management challenges for lenders without adequate hedging products to turn to—thus creating an opportunity for insurers. Ansermino (2008, 235) did not venture a forecast, but observed that "it will be interesting to see how this issue plays out."

Ansermino concluded by asserting that macroeconomic factors (especially growth in China and India) will create a boom in the commodity cycle that will result in the expansion of capacity in a number of developing countries—thus creating "demands for political risk capacity on an unprecedented scale." This will particularly be reflected in the energy sector—with the Middle East continuing to be unstable. China has been and will continue to be particularly active in trying to ensure security of supply.

Political risk mitigation has been and will continue to be a priority in structuring new investments into emerging markets. Consumers are becoming better informed and more selective in their selection of political risk investment insurance coverages. "Pricing will become more transparent and consumers will demand more sophisticated products from insurers…. users will be looking for answers to the local currency issue" (Ansermino 2008, 236)

Ansermino assumed that there will be an increase in absolute demand for political risk investment insurance coverages as well as improvements in the quality of the coverage. In the future, the private market will stretch and compete less with public sector providers—which will presage an increase in pricing. Other factors will affect the market, including the offering of guarantees by development finance institutions and the role of entities like Sinosure. There is likely to be a higher degree of cooperation between public and private insurers to use their available capacities more effectively. Traditional coverages will be reviewed, and greater scrutiny will be given to breach of contract coverage.

Reflections

Ansermino projected that development finance institutions offering guarantee products and developing countries' growing political risk investment insurance capabilities will increase supply, which will, in turn, put pressure on pricing. The effects of these developments seem to have been relatively modest and do not seem to have greatly affected political risk investment insurance pricing, but instead have made sourcing of cover somewhat more challenging and confusing. The growth of Sinosure does seem to have mitigated the projected challenge to political risk investment insurance capacity because it has supported Chinese investors' aggressive moves to secure resources. There was and is relatively little interest by Chinese investors in pursuing political risk investment insurance coverages from private insurers.

Basel II has somewhat changed the demand for political risk investment insurance coverages, but it has more directly affected the growth of the medium-term credit market. For insurers that offer both political risk investment insurance and credit, the latter is growing much faster than the former, a situation that is driven by several phenomena, but probably most significantly by Basel II.

Ansermino argued that pricing will become more transparent, which has been the case for credit cover—generally about 70 percent of bank margin. Political risk investment insurance pricing, which is still driven by a number of complex factors, seems not to have been affected. Ansermino's prediction that political risk mitigation will be a priority in structuring new extractive industry investments in emerging markets has not been manifest in dramatically increased demand for political risk investment insurance. (Local currency products and public-private cooperation have been addressed elsewhere.)

Julie Martin

As chair of the original 2006 panel on the future status of the political risk investment insurance industry in 2010, Julie Martin expanded on her oral comments at the symposium and wrote a brief paper that was included in the resulting symposium book. Reflecting her extensive experience as both an underwriter and a broker, she argued that the political risk investment insurance industry is widely misunderstood and suffers from appearing esoteric. One way for the industry to both clear up some of the misunderstanding and reduce the element of mystery is to make available more information about claims made, resolved, denied, and paid.

Greater transparency regarding claim information is hindered by concerns about confidentiality and potential adverse effects. However, Martin proposed that many of these concerns can be resolved by the aggregation and disclosure of data by the Berne Union in a format that does not compromise confidentiality issues. As of 2006, she noted that only very limited claims information had been made available by the Berne Union.

There are two important benefits resulting from more transparent disclosure about claims matters. First, the disclosure will reduce the amount of skepticism about political risk investment insurance. Brokers and underwriters who are asked whether claims have been paid in a particular country or sector are limited to their own personal knowledge because there is no credible industrywide source of information to cite. This situation can result in some investors assuming that either there is no risk or this type of insurance does not pay out, an assumption that fundamentally hurts the entire industry. Better information would dispel both of these inaccurate assumptions.

Second, consumers need to be educated about what is covered and not covered in political risk investment insurance policies. Credible information about claims matters sheds a very illuminating light that benefits both underwriters and investors. Publicly available information about claims matters allows underwriters to more credibly represent exactly what product they are selling and what it covers; the tangible interpretation of widely used policy language would make the value of political risk investment insurance clearer to both brokers and investors.

Martin argued that consumers want to know how the product works so that they can determine if it is a good fit for them. They want to know that if a politically triggered event occurs, then the coverage will respond—and how it will respond. Public disclosure of claims matters will help convince wary consumers that political risk investment insurance is both effective and responsive. The entire industry would benefit from a broader, deeper market of clients who are better informed and knowledgeable about when and where to purchase political risk investment insurance.

In general, Martin noted that the more factual the information that can be released about claims, the better it is for prospective insureds. OPIC's transparency and disclosure about claims matters has benefited many parties and is an indicator of the benefits that could occur from a broader industrywide disclosure.

Martin acknowledged that although there may be a few adverse effects to insurers from such disclosure about claims matters, the benefits will far outweigh the down side. Such disclosure will contribute to reducing skepticism and to developing a more robust industry whose product is more clearly valued.

Reflections

Although Martin fell short of making a specific forecast regarding when and how more extensive industrywide disclosure about claims matters will take place, there clearly has been some progress—as evidenced by several of this symposium's papers. With its gradually expanding membership, the Berne Union is clearly the organization best positioned to assemble and disseminate such information, but it is currently limited by its small number of staff members and the fact that not all significant political risk investment insurers are members.

It is hoped that an annual aggregate disclosure by the Berne Union on claims matters will be in a user-friendly format that will allow investors to more clearly and quickly discern the value of the political risk investment insurance product.

Although the amount of information that can be disclosed is limited by confidentiality, lessons learned also need to be shared with consumers of the product and not just among members of the Berne Union. For example, one Argentine claim denial became public, which shed light on how the claim was placed by the broker and considered by the underwriter. Several lessons drawn from this claim have been integrated into subsequent placements.

The claims process and the issues that surface regarding policy language should be shared more broadly to provide a consistent and clear basis for understanding the political risk investment insurance product.

Learning and Looking Forward

Critical Events and Developments of the Past 12 Years

Before a reflection on the lessons to be drawn from a dozen years of trying to forecast the future of the political risk investment insurance industry, it is useful, in at least in a macro sense, to note what has happened in this period.

- **Industry Players:** Over the past dozen years, there have been some new insurance entrants—both with the formation of new public entities and with some new private insurers. Some existing public sector insurers have gone through periods of "dormancy" before resuming their political risk investment insurance activities. However, the persistent number of insurers who have remained in the political risk investment insurance field should not be overlooked. Capacity has ebbed and flowed, but in general, about US$1 billion is available for any single project. The near collapse of AIG, a dominant player in many lines of insurance (including political risk investment), was noteworthy.

- **Public versus Private Insurers:** In the late 1990s, there was a fair amount of jostling, competition, and clashes between some public and private insurers as the latter sought their "rightful" place in the market. By the early 2000s, this situation had given way to increased cooperation, which was a product of many factors—accommodations by some public insurers, private insurers that focused on unserved market segments, and added public sector policy requirements that made private insurance more attractive (and whose acquisition could be accomplished with greater speed and less hassle). But at the root of this cooperation was a simple reality recognized by many industry veterans: In the political risk investment insurance area, there is more than enough risk for everyone who wants it. An insurer's success need not come at the expense of others.

- **Buyer's Market:** Much more political, economic, and financial information is readily available in the international arena, which should allow investors to better assess and manage political risks. Thanks in part to the growth in the numbers of political risk investment insurers and the stagnation in FDI flows, buyers have more political risk management alternatives now than in the early 1990s. There are more adroit, experienced underwriters and brokers available to assist investors in their risk transfer needs. The diversity of insurers allows for the possibility of procuring coverage even in poor and difficult countries. Private and public insurers have become more comfortable with various modes of coinsurance and reinsurance with one another; this works to the advantage of investors seeking coverage of large and complex projects. Compared to other forms of insurance, rates have remained reasonable.

- **Product Development:** In general, the perils covered by the political risk investment insurance industry have remained the same: inconvertibility, expropriation, political violence, and breach of contract and nonpayment. Over the years, these products have been applied to various forms of investment—such as capital markets. The core product offerings have remained stable. This stability is viewed as a strength by those who admire resiliency and a weakness by those who seek products that are more responsive to changing circumstances.

The most significant recent development, in terms of business that has been underwritten, is the coverage of credit risks of private sector entities. Although this coverage might appear to be a separate line of business, it is provided by many political risk investment insurance underwriters and will positively (or negatively) affect their ability to provide traditional political risk investment insurance coverage. Although the lines are blurred, the distinction seems to be that payment risk of a private sector entity is a credit risk, but the same coverage of a public sector entity is a political risk.

The "sparks" in product development of political risk investment insurance seem to have great difficulty in "catching fire" and becoming major industry innovations. Certainly, the swift private insurance initiative in writing stand-alone terrorism coverage was noteworthy. But the failure of OPIC's liquidity devaluation product to catch on and the difficulty of covering intellectual property rights despite the demand for these products seem to be more typical.

Looking Back at the Forecasts of the Future of the Political Risk Investment Insurance Industry

In the beginning of this paper, it was suggested that the challenge of trying to steer down a mountain road in a vehicle with a mud-covered windshield might be a relevant metaphor for the political risk investment insurance industry. Looking back and understanding where one has been is important (the rearview mirror), but so is trying to peer forward through a murky windshield. Moreover, one should not ignore many other factors—the equivalent of using one's peripheral vision to pick up useful information about the perils ahead, the "sound and feel" of the road, and a poised foot cautiously resting on the brake pedal—that can contribute to successful navigation of a dangerous road.

Metaphors aside, it is useful to remind ourselves why we try to forecast at all—regardless of the industry. If one *underestimates* the market of the future, one can suffer from lost sales opportunities, dissatisfied customers, insufficient resources to meet demand, and the high likelihood of missing significant market turns. If one *overestimates* the market, one can suffer from underused resources, wasteful costs, and reduced cash flow. (In the case of public sector entities, one might say that—either because of underestimating or overestimating the market—they failed to achieve a mission in an optimal fashion.) In either case of *mis-estimation*, the credibility of management suffers and an opportunity is lost for managers to demonstrate their competency and improve their understanding of the business.

Reviewing more than 80 papers written over a 12-year period by experts in a somewhat esoteric field of political risk investment insurance is a humbling experience. It is clearly difficult enough for anyone in the political risk investment insurance field to understand the current situation, much less to attempt to forecast the future—when in doing so one might be subject to the proverbial "slings and arrows" of superiors, subordinates, and peers. The personal rewards of forecasting the future do not seem commensurate with the personal risks. Yet it obviously needs to be done.

The political risk investment insurance industry is not alone with respect to having difficulty foreseeing future developments; this case is true in many fields. However, articulating the specific difficulties faced by participants in this industry when looking into the future is worth noting. The limitations include the following:

1. The paucity of historical data, systematically collected, on an industry basis precludes many types of analysis. In particular, data on claims and recoveries are lacking. Although one knows one's own firm's experience, counterpart data from other entities can only be crudely estimated. (Hence, there were pleas from many individuals over the years for the Berne Union to take a leadership role in the area of providing statistics.)
2. Even if systematic insurance claims loss data were available, it would only partially capture the extent of investment losses that have occurred. Because the overwhelming majority of FDI into emerging and developing markets is uninsured, total political risk losses are unknown. Hence, most of the recent nationalizations in Venezuela were of investors who did not have coverage. (This was also the case in Iran in the 1970s and Cuba in the 1950s.)
3. The diversity of eligibility and policy criteria that restrict the activities of many political risk investment insurers has created a nonhomogeneous industry. The presence of national, multilateral, and private insurers, as well as of various kinds of financial guarantees, contributes to a complexity problem. (Hence, the argument from some that the political risk investment insurance industry isn't even a business (Ascari 2010).)
4. The small size of the political risk investment insurance industry relative to other insurance sectors means that it is particularly vulnerable to factors and events in other sectors (especially in obtaining reinsurance). In addition, in some large private insurers, political risk investment insurance underwriters have a sense of isolation from the mainstream of their organization's business.

In some public sector entities, there is a similar sense of isolation in the face of much larger trade-related business.

5. Estimating the effects of adverse selection and "competition" from self-insurance is particularly problematic as one tries to look into the future. What assumptions are reasonable to make about the risk management practices of state-owned enterprises or sovereign wealth funds? Are such entities likely to self-insure? Or will they rely only on national insurers?

6. The implicit—or occasionally explicit—effects of these limitations means that industry participants are most comfortable in talking about the present situation and, occasionally, in identifying what trends are likely to continue, what trends are likely to change, and what is novel. Although these topics are certainly welcomed by most industry participants, they usually fall short of any type of holistic or systemic view of the political risk investment insurance industry. Hence, industrywide analyses are rarely undertaken (and made public) unless there is an unusual stimulus. For example, the creation of MIGA in the late 1980s occasioned such a review, as did the entry of a new reinsurer (Swiss Re) to the political risk investment insurance market.

Certainly as part of internal budgetary or legislative reviews, many of the national and multilateral agencies regularly produce internal estimations of future business in terms of "high, low, and likely outcomes" or "possible, probable, or preferred outcomes." In slightly modified fashion, some private insurers also undertake such annual reviews. These forecasts tend to state their fundamental assumptions and then vary certain other factors under their control (for example, budget size, personnel numbers, and so on). A rigorous "alternative futures" analysis is rarely undertaken (in part because of the limitations noted previously).

As a result, little rigorous attention tends to be given to the potential sources of bias that even "armchair [political risk investment insurance] forecasters" need to guard against. From our review of these articles from previous symposia, there seem to be four sources of bias that are of particular note:

1. *Recency bias:* The tendency to use only the most recent events when extrapolating trends into the future; the latest "big" event is not always a "turning point"

2. *Optimism bias:* The tendency to succumb to the innate bias (that psychologists tell us that we all have) to be optimistic

3. *Bureaucratic or political bias:* The tendency, stemming from an acute awareness of the internal dynamics of one's organization, to hew to an institutional position or to one's boss's position

4. *Cynicism bias:* The tendency (usually implicit) to view nearly all forecasts as futile; the view that any one institution—and perhaps the industry collectively—is a "cork in the ocean" whose path is shaped by macro forces beyond anyone's knowledge or control

Drawing Lessons from Past Forecasting Efforts: Practical Foresight and Humility

It is obvious that the political risk investment insurance industry (and the individual entities composing it) is buffeted by many trends, uncertainties, and challenges that are difficult to understand. It is also clear that there is considerable evidence of greater rather than lesser prospects for global, regional, and national disruptions and shocks in the future. Hence, forecasting methods that rely heavily on past patterns (for which the political risk investment insurance industry has precious little data) are less likely to be relevant in foreseeing what will happen tomorrow and when it will happen. In a world with seemingly growing complexity and ambiguity as to what will happen, one needs to pause and address the basic question: *What then is to be done?*

A business guru might generically reply that what is needed is a nimble, resilience-focused, forward-thinking organization that has learned to identify emerging trends and "tipping points" so as to help them flourish in an ever-more-competitive and complex world. Although superficially appealing, that abstract level of response contains little in terms of practical, actionable steps for members of the political risk investment insurance industry. So one might ask: *What practically is to be done?* It is useful to address that question by differentiating between short-term actions and longer-term actions.

In the long term, the foundation should be building an organization with wider global knowledge obtained from many more external sources and adequate (if not enhanced) cognitive skills to chart the organization's best future course. In particular, a political risk investment insurer needs to have leadership and a staff that seeks mastery of the following skills:

1. *Trend assessment:* The competency to understand the current and immediate future trend directions, to assess their likely effect on one another, and to respond in a timely and appropriate manner
2. *Pattern recognition:* The ability to see patterns rather than just individual factors; the ability to identify important anomalies
3. *System perspective:* The capability to see the entire insurance and reinsurance system rather than individual pieces (that is, to see the "big picture")
4. *Anticipatory capabilities:* The ability not only to identify trends and patterns and to understand the system, but also to anticipate the short- and long-term consequences of those trends and patterns over time
5. *Logic and instinct:* The willingness to rely on a combination of logic and instinct (especially when purely rational data analysis is so difficult to undertake)

Organizations that enable and encourage their people to develop these competencies (or "foresight skills") can acquire and maintain a sustainable future-oriented edge in the marketplace. The absence of these competencies obviously dooms an organization to failure.

Public sector political risk insurers face a particular challenge in dealing with the periodic upheaval of their top management as a result of changes in administrations. It is rare that the new leadership has any experience in the insurance industry, or perhaps even in international business. This situation places an enormous burden on the senior civil servants to successfully communicate the esoteric nature of the political risk investment insurance business and to cooperate in bringing the new management up to speed. In parallel fashion, there is an enormous need for the new political leadership to have initial confidence in the existing managers and to learn the business quickly. If there is failure in either case, stagnation or decline is likely.

In the short term, there are obviously specific actions that must be taken within each political risk investment insurer to address specific shortcomings previously identified. These actions may take place in recruitment, training, marketing, underwriting, or management. Because of the uniqueness of these actions to each organization, they are impossible to identify in a paper such as this. However, there are some generic short-term actions that can be described.

Reactive versus Proactive Mindset

Many previous symposium participants have pointed with pride to the industry's history of *reactive* adaptation to new challenges, including the swift development of a stand-alone terrorism coverage and their ability to "stretch" some existing coverages into novel new uses. A certain behavioral mode of insurers responding to brokers and buyers that push for a new application of traditional coverages to new circumstances has become the norm. However, there is a "dark side" to this mindset. It is considered "normal" to be reactive. Many insurers lack a *proactive* tradition of investing in research and new product development in anticipation of fulfilling investor needs. This proactive mindset is not an alternative to the reactive mode, but an addition to it. Therefore, it is useful to retrospectively ask questions: Was the industry response to Basel II prompt and adequate? Could the industry have better anticipated the needs of investors? Then one is better positioned to address the question: *What should the industry do to better respond to the opportunities created by Basel III?*

Opportunities abound for more tailored political risk investment insurance coverages for certain sectors. One need not be an international economist to know that oil and gas exploration and development is a sector that has attracted and will continue to attract a great deal of investment in emerging markets over the next decade. Why has so little of this investment been covered by political risk insurers historically? Is it because the insurers have not invested in the development of appropriate contract language? The same can be said of intellectual property rights coverages, which have intermittently been explored by a few insurers over the past 20 years, but have not yet yielded an appealing product. The point is that a less *reactive* and more *proactive* mindset is likely to open new avenues for growth for insurers who are willing to devote the staff time to develop new applications of traditional products.

Berne Union

In the short term, the potential benefit to Berne Union's members for it to collect and disseminate important information from those members for the benefit of those members is difficult to overestimate. Hammering out agreements with respect to what data are collected, how they are collected, how they are aggregated to protect confidential information, and when they are to be collected is always difficult in multilateral entities or associations. Moreover, there is no shortcut to the labor-intensive nature of the task—which at its core requires an initial set of political decisions by its members. And although forging consensus is always desirable, a time may come when the benefits foregone induce a majority subset of the members to decide to pool specified information among themselves and—while sharing it among themselvesdeny it to the minority who are unwilling or unable to contribute information to the process. (In other fields, this has produced a successful outcome.)

Originating and Disseminating Information about the Political Risk Investment Insurance Industry

Individual underwriters and brokers have websites and brochures, and they regularly attempt to market their political risk investment insurance services in other ways. However, there is a general paucity of information that dispassionately analyzes and comments on political risk investment insurance industry developments. Articles heightening awareness of the industry's capabilities and specific, innovative, precedent-setting deals (especially those written by a user of industry coverages) benefit everyone in the industry. Articles published in academic, legal, business, insurance, banking, and accounting professional journals about political risk investment insurance are of particular benefit. Creative, junior staff members at political risk investment insurers, perhaps guided by their more senior colleagues, should be encouraged to write for such journals. In the same spirit, case studies that detail exactly how innovative financing and investment insurance can work together to enhance the feasibility and viability of a project are exceptionally valuable.

A Concluding Thought

Notwithstanding the previously mentioned possible short- and long-term actions that might be taken, one should recall that by its nature the insurance business is inherently conservative—and that this quality is one of its strengths. Warren Buffet has reportedly said that the insurance business is a very simple business in which one can be very successful if one strictly follows three simple rules:

1. Underwrite prudently.
2. Operate and invest prudently.
3. Don't do anything else. The third rule is the most important, is the most difficult to follow, and is the reason—if violated—that insurance companies tend to get in trouble.

Epilogue

Every year brings new individuals to the political risk investment insurance industry. One of the passions these individuals tend to have is a desire to bring greater rigor and rationality (or science) to bear on the challenge of balancing the risk transfer needs of investors with the prudent risk assumptions needs of insurers. Often they come equipped with new statistical, economic, or legal insights that will "solve" the extant problems. Although such new blood (and new thinking) is always welcomed, it does bring to mind the story of the young systems engineer-turned-pilot who was flying North Pacific routes.

Dismayed at the unscientific approaches of older pilots, he developed a complex model based on years of data involving hundreds of variables to plot how to "optimally" fly the Tokyo–to–San Francisco route. Although older pilots were skeptical, the young pilot was allowed to load the model into the plane's computer and, setting the plane on autopilot, he confidently flew the route— only to end up in San Francisco Bay about 200 meters short of the runway. Rescue workers found the pilot strapped into his seat, still smiling broadly. When asked why he was so happy after crashing the plane, he cheerfully noted that considering he flew all the way from Tokyo, 200 meters was not much of an error. Moreover, he noted that he was on schedule and had minimized fuel consumption!

This story contains a number of insights for those in the political risk investment insurance industry. First, however scientific one's underwriting system, relying solely on it (as on an autopilot) is foolish—especially when timely human intervention can help avoid a catastrophe. Second, one should be wary of making precise forecasts too far in advance when circumstances can change. (In this case, when leaving Tokyo the pilot could have selected a general route and adjusted the course as conditions changed—especially near the end). Clearly, considering all the uncertainties, one's forecasts should not extend beyond what is prudent—especially when one will acquire new information in due course. Third and finally, rigor and rationality can bring considerable benefits, but if one wants a successful career (either in flying or in political risk investment insurance underwriting), good judgment and common sense still matter.An experienced pilot could have easily been able to combine the expertise of the young pilot in terms of timeliness and fuel savings with a few prudent last-minute adjustments to successfully complete the flight.

BIBLIOGRAPHY

Ascari, Raoul. 2010. "Political Risk Insurance: An Industry in Search of a Business." Working Paper 12, SACE, Rome.

Anserimo, Greg, 2008. "The Scramble for New Commodities: Medium-Term Trends in Political Risk Insurance" in *International Political Risk Management: Needs of the Present, Challenges for the Future*, Theodore H. Moran, Gerald T. West and Keith Martin, 225–237, World Bank.

Brown, Vivian. 2004. "Political Risk Insurance after September 11 and the Argentine Crisis: A Public Provider's Perspective." In *International Political Risk Management: The Brave New World*, edited by Theodore H. Moran, 15–25. Washington, DC: World Bank.

Churchill, Winston L. 1947. *The Official Report of the House of Commons*. 5th series, Vol. 444, 206–07, November 11.

Díaz-Cassou, Javier, Aitor Erce-Domínguez, and Juan J. Vázquez-Zamora. 2008. *Recent Episodes of Sovereign Debt Restructurings. A Case-Study Approach*. Documentos Ocasionales No. 0804, Banco de España, Madrid.

Duperreault, Brian. 2004. "In the Aftermath of September 11 and the Argentine Crisis: A Private Reinsurer's Perspective." In *International Political Risk Management: The Brave New World*, edited by Theodore H. Moran, 45–52. Washington, DC: World Bank.

Gaillard, Emmanuel. 2003. "l'Arbitrage sur le fondement des traités de protection des investissements: Les états dans le contentieux économique international, I. Le contentieux arbitral." *Revue de l'Arbitrage* 3: 853–59.

———. 2005. "Investment Treaty Arbitration and Jurisdiction over Contract Claims: The SGS Cases Considered." In *International Investment Law and Arbitration: Leading Cases from the ICSID, NAFTA, Bilateral Treaties, and Customary International Law*, edited by Todd Weiler, 325–46. London: Cameron May.

———. 2007. "The Denunciation of the ICSID Convention." *New York Law Journal*, June 26: 7.

———. 2009. "Identify or Define? Reflections on the Evolution of the Concept of Investment in ICSID Practice." In *International Investment Law for the 21st Century: Essays in Honour of Cristoph Schreuer*, edited by Christina Binder, Ursula Kriebaum, August Reinisch, and Stephan Wittich, 403–16. London: Oxford University Press.

———. 2010. *La Jurisprudence du CIRDI*. Vol. 2. Paris: Éditions A. Pedone.

Gallagher London. 2010. "Political Risks Insurance Report and Market Update July 2010." Gallagher London, London.

GNA (Ghana News Agency). 2010. "Gov't Pays Down Tema Oil Refinery's Debt to Ghana Commercial Bank." *Cedi Post*, March 24. http://www.cedipost.com/business/govt-pays-down-tema-oil-refinerys-debt-to-ghana-commercial-bank.html.

Heppel, Toby. 2005. "Perspectives on Private-Public Relationships in Political Risk Insurance." In *International Political Risk Management: Looking to the Future*, edited by Theodore H. Moran and Gerald T. West, 139–57. Washington, DC: World Bank.

James, David. 2004. "Political Risk Insurance after September 11 and the Argentine Crisis: An Underwriter's View from London." In *International Political Risk Management: The Brave New World*, edited by Theodore H. Moran, 26–38. Washington, DC: World Bank.

Judiciary of England and Wales. 2007. "Report and Recommendations of the Commercial Court Long Trials Working Party." Judiciary of England and Wales, London.

Kinnear, Meg. 2011. "The Future of ICSID?" Presentation at the Fifth Annual Investment Treaty Arbitration Conference, Washington, DC, April 5.

Konrad, Sabine. 2007. "Comments on 'Investment Protection by Other Mechanisms: The Role of Human Rights Institutions and the World Trade Organization' by Christina Pfaff." In *The International Convention on Settlement Disputes: Taking Stock after 40 Years*, edited by Rainer Hofmann and Christian Tams, 323–24. Sinzheim, Germany: Nomos Publishers.

———. 2008. "Investitionsschutz." In *Rechtshandbuch Projektfinanzierung und PPP: Vertragsgestaltung und Projektdurchführung nach deutschem Recht unter Berücksichtigung internationaler Erfahrungen*, edited by Ulf R. Siebel, Jan-Hendrik Röver, and Christian Knütel, 321–70. Cologne, Munich: Carl Heymanns Verlag.

Martin, Julie. 2004. "Commentary on Political Risk Insurance Providers in the Aftermath of September 11 and the Argentine Crisis." In *International Political Risk Management: The Brave New World*, edited by Theodore H. Moran, 53–66. Washington, DC: World Bank.

Marwick, Sandy. 1998. "Trends in Political Risk for Corporate Investors." In *Managing International Political Risk*, edited by Theodore H. Moran, 44–56. Malden, MA: Blackwell Publishers.

McIlwrath, Michael, and John Savage. 2010. *International Arbitration and Mediation: A Practical Guide*. Alphen aan den Rijn, Netherlands: Wolters Kluwer.

MIGA (Multilateral Investment Guarantee Agency). 2010. *World Investment and Political Risk 2009*. Washington, DC: World Bank.

Moran, Theodore H., ed. 1998. *Managing International Political Risk*. Malden, MA: Blackwell Publishers.

———. 2004. *International Political Risk Management: The Brave New World*. Washington, DC: World Bank.

Moran, Theodore H., and Gerald T. West, eds. 2005. *International Political Risk Management: Looking to the Future*. Washington, DC: World Bank.

Moya, Elena. 2009. "Six Dubai Companies Downgraded to Junk Status." *Guardian*, December 8. http://www.guardian.co.uk/business/2009/dec/08/dubai-companies-downgraded-rating-action.

Ngo Khac Le. 2010. "Vinashin: Lessons Learned." *Baird Maritime*, August 24. http://www.bairdmaritime.com/index.php?option=com_content&view=article&id=7698:vinashin-lessons-learned&catid=113:ports-and-shipping&Itemid=208&q=lessons+learned.

O'Sullivan, Robert. 2004. "Learning from OPIC's Experience with Claims and Arbitration." Paper presented at MIGA-Georgetown Symposium on International Political Risk Management, Washington, DC, November 12.

OECD (Organisation for Economic Co-operation and Development). 2004. "Fair and Equitable Treatment Standard in International Investment Law." Working Papers on International Investment 2004/3, OECD, Paris.

———. 2006. "Interpretation of the Umbrella Clause in Investment Agreements." Working Papers on International Investment 2006/3, OECD, Paris.

Palmer, Joanne. 2008. "Looking Ahead: Will Political Risk Insurance Continue to Play a Meaningful Role in the Global Investment and Trade Environment?" In *International Political Risk Management: Needs of the Present, Challenges for the Future*, edited by Theodore H. Moran, Gerald T. West, and Keith Martin, 215–24. Washington, DC: World Bank.

Powers, Linda F. 1998. "New Forms of Protection for International Infrastructure Investors." In *Managing International Political Risk*, edited by Theodore H. Moran, 125–38. Malden, MA: Blackwell Publishers.

Radelet, Steven. 1999. "Orderly Workouts for Cross-Border Private Debt." Harvard Institute for International Development, Cambridge, MA.

Riordan, Daniel W., and Edward A. Coppola. 2005. "Currency Transfer and Convertibility Coverage: An Old Reliable Product or Just an Old Product?" In *International Political Risk Management: Looking to the Future*, edited by Theodore H. Moran and Gerald T. West, 182–92. Washington, DC: World Bank.

Salinger, John. 1998. "The Future of Private Political Risk Insurance." In *Managing International Political Risk*, edited by Theodore H. Moran, 169–72. Malden, MA: Blackwell Publishers.

———. 2004. "The Impact of September 11 on Trade Credit and Political Risk Insurance: A Private Insurer's Perspective from New York." In *International Political Risk Management: The Brave New World*, edited by Theodore H. Moran, 39–44. Washington, DC: World Bank.

———. 2008. "Past and Future Predictions for the Political Risk Insurance Industry." In *International Political Risk Management: Needs of the Present, Challenges for the Future*, edited by Theodore H. Moran, Gerald T. West, and Keith Martin, 201–08. Washington, DC: World Bank.

Schreuer, Christoph H., Loretta Malintoppi, August Reinisch, and Anthony Sinclair. 2009. *The ICSID Convention: A Commentary*. 2nd ed. Cambridge, UK: Cambridg Press.

Schroeder, Alice. 2008. *The Snowball: Warren Buffett and the Business of Life*. New York: Bantam Books.

Simons, Bright B., and Franklin Cudjoe. 2009. "Unravelling Ghana State-Owned Oil Refinery (TOR) Debt: A Provisional Analysis." AfricanLiberty.org, January 27. http://africanliberty.org/node/595.

Steinglass, Matt. 2010. "Arrests at Vietnam's State Shipbuilder Worry Its Foreign Investors." *Financial Times* (blog), September 20. http://blogs.ft.com/beyond-brics/2010/09/20/arrests-at-vietnams-state-shipbuilder-worry-its-foreign-investors/.

S&P (Standard and Poor's). 2009a. "Enhanced Methodology and Assumptions for Rating Government-Related Entities." *Global Credit Portal Ratings Direct*, June 29.

———. 2009b. "What Factors May Affect S&P's View of the Likelihood of Extraordinary Government Support for Dubai-Based GREs?" *Global Credit Portal Ratings Direct*, October 15.

Teather, David. 2009. "Dubai Government Washes Its Hands of $59bn Debt Built Up by Dubai World." *Guardian*, November 30. http://www.guardian.co.uk/world/2009/nov/30/dubai-government-debt-pile.

Think Ghana. 2010. "Bailout Package for Tema Oil Refinery." Lyon Media Limited, Ghana, March 16. http://business.thinkghana.com/news/201003/46453.php.

Tobin, Clive. 2005. "The Future of the International Political Risk Insurance Industry." In *International Political Risk Management: Looking to the Future*, edited by Theodore H. Moran and G. T. West, 128–38. Washington, DC: World Bank.

UN (United Nations). 1997. *World Investment Report 1997: Transnational Corporations, Market Structure and Competition Policy*. Geneva: United Nations.

Viet Nam Business News. 2010. "Vietnam's Vinashin Finishes Natixis Debt Repayment." October 1. http://businesstimes.com.vn/vietnams-vinashin-finishes-natixis-debt-repayment/.

Wearden, Graeme. 2009. "Dubai World Will Repay Its Debts, UAE Economy Minister Insists." *Guardian*, December 3. http://www.guardian.co.uk/business/2009/dec/03/dubai-world-financial-crisis.

Wells, Lou. 1998. "God and Fair Competition: Does the Foreign Direct Investor Face Still Other Risks in Emerging Markets?" In *Managing International Political Risk*, edited by Theodore H. Moran, 15–43. Malden, MA: Blackwell Publishers.

West, Gerald T. 2004. "Political Risk Investment Insurance: The International Market and MIGA." In *International Political Risk Management: The Brave New World*, edited by Theodore H. Moran, 192–216. Washington, DC: World Bank.

West, Gerald T., and Keith Martin. 2001. "Political Risk Investment Insurance: The Renaissance Revisited." In *International Political Risk Management: Exploring New Frontiers*, edited by T. Moran, 207–30. Washington, DC: World Bank.

West, Gerald T., and Kristopher Hamel. 2005. "Whither the Political Risk Insurance Industry?" In *International Political Risk Management: Looking to the Future*, edited by Theodore H. Moran and Gerald T. West, 206–30. Washington, DC: World Bank.

Westholm-Schröder, Christina. 2005. "The Use of Political Risk Insurance to Support Emerging Market-Based Issuers." In *International Political Risk Management: Looking to the Future*, edited by Theodore H. Moran and Gerald T. West, 173–81. Washington, DC: World Bank.

———. 2008. "How Will the Political Risk Insurance Industry Evolve in the Next Three to Five Years?" In *International Political Risk Management: Needs of the Present, Challenges for the Future*, edited by Theodore H. Moran, Gerald T. West, and Keith Martin, 209–14. Washington, DC: World Bank.

Zawya.com. 2010. "Dubai World's Finalisation of Debt Restructuring Is Positive for UAE Banks." Press Release from Moody's Investors Service, September 13. http://www.zawya.com/story.cfm/sidZAWYA20100913094238.

www.ingramcontent.com/pod-product-compliance
Lightning Source LLC
Chambersburg PA
CBHW081508200326
41518CB00015B/2422